Transformation

A Journey from Abuser to Advocate

W. E. COMMODORE

PAGE PUBLISHING, INC.
Conneaut Lake, PA

First originally published by Page Publishing 2021

ISBN 978-1-6624-1460-2 (pbk)
ISBN 978-1-6624-1461-9 (digital)

Printed in the United States of America

CHAPTER

One

My soul made its entrance into this world through a horrific act of domestic violence demonstrated by the behaviors of an out-of-control husband who had "trust issues" with his pregnant wife.

My father worked the 11:00 p.m. to 7:00 a.m. shift at Honeywell, and he decided to "pop in" on his wife on his lunch break at 3:00 a.m. As he quietly entered the residence, he opened the door to see his wife lying in Murphy bed that folded into the closet. After careful inspection of the condition of the place, he began to complain in an accusatory manner that there were dirty dishes in the sink, the stove hadn't been wiped, and the floor wasn't swept. When his wife apologized and told him of her stomach pains, he confronted her with the fact that she was only six months along and was feigning illness to avoid her *matrimonial* duties.

She could only sit there and cry as he cursed her weak responses, and in one violent act of rage, he folded my mother and the bed into the closet, slammed the door, and stormed back to work. Lunch break was over!

My father slammed the door to the apartment so hard that a neighbor heard the noise and saw the apartment door ajar. Then heard her screams from the closet and aided her in getting her out.

In fifteen minutes, my mother was rushed to Northwestern Hospital on Twenty-Fifth and Chicago in Minneapolis. The delivery was very easy and uncomplicated because at two pounds thirteen ounces, I wasn't very massive. My mother would describe her delivery as one of "spitting me out."

I went directly into an incubator, and my mother was told by Dr. Lawrence F. Richdorf, the pediatrician, that "the child might not live through the night."

At noon the same day, Mom was at the door waiting for her two cousins Phillip and Doris to pick her up and drive her to Excelsior Amusement Park.

In fairness to Mom, she was in a state of trauma and shock after what she'd been through and no husband in sight…

CHAPTER

Two

I spent quite some time in an incubator because of my size at birth, and at the six-month mark, the doctors discovered that although my blood type was compatible with my mother's (O positive), I was dying from it and required a complete blood transfusion. My father (biological) submitted his (O negative) blood, and I made a remarkable recovery. Years later when I looked at my photo at one year old, I was a healthy baby with a bald head from the shaving at the time of the transfusion, as it had to be done through my head.

I would go home at some point but soon returned to St. Barnabus Hospital with double pneumonia and then another visit in a couple weeks after discharge for another bout of double pneumonia and an extended stay.

I remember my grandmother (on my father's side) coming every day in each case, and I remember looking out the window and seeing my twin uncles down below waiting outside, because at their age of seven, they couldn't come up to my room.

Ironically, I have no memories of any of my hospital stay's visitors other than my grandmother. I'm sure I had more visitors, but my emotional connection was with my grandmother. Each time she walked in the room with the love and kindness in her greeting, "How's my little guy?" I would respond with "Hi, Guy!"

Her birth name was Sara Aleatha Lee Commodore. She was born in Hannibal, Missouri, and came to Minneapolis from La Grange, Illinois, at eighteen years old with her older brother named Pascal Jr. Their father was from New Orleans, Louisiana. My grandmother was my earliest introduction to unconditional love that I can remember. I have no real memories of my mother or father except for their violent exchanges, and in each case the aftermath found me revisiting the emergency room of several hospitals either trauma-tized or injured and sometimes both, as my father was undeniably destructive and vicious in his attacks of my mother and me. He had no understanding of my value as his infant son, only that I was in his space when he was reprimanding his *woman*.

My father was loud, explosive, and physically violent. In some cases, he was known to throw a plate of food to the ceiling because it was too cold.

In one instance during one of his tirades, I was thrown through the air and hit the refrigerator, and I remember waking up in a hos-pital room.

A little before I turned two years of age, my father had his last act of domestic violence with my mother.

She was pregnant once again, and because of his trust issues he beat her up. When I tried to protect her, he threw me through the air, and this time I hit my chin on the metal guardrail on my bed. He then proceeded to stomp my mother's stomach to destroy the fetus of whoever the "other man was." My brother Stephen Commodore lived twenty-three days, and the official cause of death was yellow jaundice.

I woke up in another hospital, only this time I had polio. In those days, they put you in what was called an iron lung, which was my home for a while. I don't remember much about that experience except that the Minneapolis Laker basketball team paid me a visit and gave me an autographed ball.

The one memory that I do have is the braces on my legs and dragging myself around on the floor. It was during that period when my mother was dating Willie Mays, who at that time was playing baseball for the Minneapolis Millers, a farm team for the New York Giants.

Mom was also dating a few other men, including a man who would become my stepfather. Mom was very beautiful to look at and the fact that she had attended charm school gave her an additional trait in her list of qualifications.

I don't have many memories of a relationship with my mother, but I can remember her meanness—it was more of a feeling of never being connected.

To understand my environmental conditions in the 1940s, in Minneapolis I was thought of as a member of the colored race, as we were referred to then. The most important fact about the colored population in Minnesota was its small size. The 1910 census bureau counted just 7,084 colored in a population of more than two million.

While Detroit's population increased sixfold and Cleveland threefold during World War I, the Twin Cities saw only a 50 percent increase. By 1940, some 4,646 colored lived in Minneapolis, which was 0.09 percent of the total population.

While 4,139 lived in St. Paul, 1.5 percent of that city's population, between 1940 and 1950, Minnesota's colored population rose to 14,022, a 41 percent increase.

My point is that it's a very small amount of colored cultural expression that affects the masses of "other people."

My parents were both born in Minneapolis. They were both from families who came from Louisiana. Her family was from Cotton Valley and his from New Orleans.

My father, after returning from leave in the Navy, married my mother when she was seventeen years old at the time, and he was eighteen years old.

During this war and after war period, the colored servicemen had a completely different social mindset than others.

The colored soldiers saw a segregated and lower-tier military experience, certainly a test of their character. My father was a Baker First Class, and that was about all that he ever told me about his four years in the Navy.

After enlisting at seventeen years of age, he married my mother and returned from service, and the follies began.

Mother was seeing my father and future stepfather at the same time, as it was the culture of the colored people of that generation in the Twin Cities in those times. Monogamy was of very little social value. The men weren't loyal to their mates, and most of the mates weren't faithful either. In the Twin Cities, this was the Jody Period—players who swoop in and your wife, girlfriend, or mate is gone…

This act of relationship infringement seemed not only the mentality of this small colored society. I was born into this colored culture in the Twin Cities, and my mother, father, and stepfather were masters of deception in this era of seeing multiple partners, as is called dating today.

The problem with this sport was that there was an unspoken nondisclosure clause, which some who thought they had a monogamous relationship were sadly disappointed, to say the least.

My father was considered a smooth player with looks, charm, and style. My future stepfather was smooth, charming and had good looks and style. He was six feet and one and a half inches tall on a well-muscled two-hundred-pound frame. He was an accomplished boxer in the Navy as well, with a heavyweight record of 38-0.

My mother, father, and stepfather grew up in South Minneapolis, and my stepfather was two years older than my father and three years older than my mother. Both men were best friends, and since my father was smaller in stature (five feet and ten inches and 155 pounds) and two years younger than my stepfather, he looked up to his friend as his big brother. My mother told me late in life that in hard times my stepfather, his mother, and sister lived with them at her parents' home for a period.

The three members of the triangle (Father, Mother, Stepfather) were not strangers to one another. They would be interconnected for my entire life. This stepfather began raising me at two years of age and will be from now on referred to as my *dad*.

The real player in the game of love was my mom, who was controlling the players. By the time I got out of my twos, my mother had divorced my father, married my dad, and they were living in a high-rise apartment on the South Side of Chicago. I was living with Mother Young in Minneapolis. It seems that a group of Masons paid my Eastern Star member Grandmother (Ella, my dad's mother) a visit to encourage her son to leave town until further notice!

I remember Mother Young's house vividly because her livelihood was taking in other people's laundry. I spent the day listening to

Arthur Godfrey on the radio and watching her wash, fold, iron, etc. She was elderly but very cheerful. I remember my mother and dad coming back to town at Christmas and making me leave the room, and someone got up on the roof of the house and made reindeer noises and I was led back to see the Christmas tree all full of toys under it.

Not long afterward, I was living with them in that high-rise in Chicago. My only memories I have there are of riding on the elevator and washing someone's socks in a nut bowl and got a whipping for it.

My next memories are the Sumner Field projects in North Minneapolis.

My strangest memory is the laundry room where my grand-mother (Guy) did her laundry. My mother and I lived in those projects, but I spent most of my time with my grandmother. Some of my earliest friendships were with other kids living in those projects. One memory was of all the people that sat out in front on parade chairs all day and night just talking and commenting on life in a seg-regated Minneapolis. I remember Saturday night when the popcorn man would pull up and everyone ran and lined up to get popcorn, push-up sticks, and other types of goodies.

Before long I was living at 313 Humboldt Avenue North in Minneapolis in a downstairs section of a duplex. I was going to Phyllis Wheatley Nursery School, where my teacher Ms. Bertha Smith was the motherly love that I didn't have outside my grandmother Guy.

My most outstanding memory was the day my playmate KO (Kenneth Wallace) got off the teeter-totter with me at the top, leav-ing me to slam to the ground, and in the process I bit through the middle of my tongue. Blood went everywhere. An ambulance came and rushed me to General Hospital, and I spent weeks drinking all my meals through a straw.

CHAPTER

Three

Kindergarten was for the most part uneventful, with an exception of my sixth birthday at the close of the school year. That morning my mother and I had a discussion that led to me calling her a mean brat. I got my mouth washed out with Coco Castile soap, which tasted terrible, and I remember dragging my tongue along my bedspread to get the taste off my tongue to no avail and drinking a sip of water made me sick. To make matters worse, Mom took me to school with three boxes of cupcakes to share with my classmates as a birthday celebration. Teacher Bennett opened the boxes of cupcakes while my mother announced that there would be no birthday party because I called her a brat. That did not go over very well with my classmates, but my mother relented, and everyone got to eat cupcakes while I watched as punishment. Other than naptime and recess, we had auditorium visitors. The most outstanding visitor was Officer Sevanich. Everyone loved him.

During first grade, Ms. Cecil and I had a clash of personalities that had me at the beginning of incorrigible behavior. I had a speech impediment and went to speech class with other kids with speaking deficiencies. Ms. Cecil was an "old battle-ax" that was always spitting into a Kleenex and putting it into her pocket on her sweater. I must have been way out of line because she punched me in the chest with her fist out in the hallway and made me stand outside the classroom. By spring of the next year, I wasn't going to school at Harrison Elementary at all because I'd leave home and hide under a car in the vacant lot next to our duplex and go home at the end of the day like it was just a normal day.

My parents (Mom and Dad) were absorbed with my one-year-old sister, who bonded their marriage, and I became a dangling appendage. Ms. Cecil never reported my absences, but my report card was full of Ns (for Needs Improvement) and very few Ss (Satisfactory). I was clearly showing signs of troubled behavior, but my parents were so self-absorbed that they didn't have a clue.

My parents were everyday drinkers and had house parties on the weekends, where company was loud and it was hard to sleep in the bedroom. From time to time my dad would slap my mother, and she'd go down and get in the car and drive off crying. At six years of age, I didn't know what to do. I also remember the windows were open and I heard my mother yell, "Bob [Dad], I think my jaw is broken!" She then came running outside, got in the car, and drove off.

The environmental conditions were showing in my behavior at school because by second grade, I was being suspended for my odd behavior. My teacher Ms. Adams was the very pretty, loving daughter of radio television personality and *Star Tribune* (Minneapolis daily paper) columnist Cedric Adams. Ms. Adams didn't deserve to have a child like me in her classroom, but I was troubled. On one occasion, I was in big trouble for comparing penises with Robert Lewis in line at an auditorium entrance. Ms. Adams saw me exposing myself, and I was suspended. I got home with the note and was promptly given a whipping. I remember requesting a hand whipping instead of my behind because my hands were the guilty party.

On another occasion, Ms. Adams placed me and my desk in the coatroom, and I barricaded both entrances so the kids could not go home for lunch. I was incorrigible in the worst way, but my parents were so charming that no one could understand where these behaviors were coming from.

Somehow, I graduated into third grade with Mr. Polance as my teacher, and while I wasn't acting out, I was acting up in class. There was a girl that sat next to me in class named Peggy who asked me if I wanted to feel her behind. She took my hand and put it inside her panties and just left it there for the duration of the class period. As a matter of fact, Peggy came in every day for about two weeks and placed my hand in her underwear. I'd just sit there like that each day and didn't have a clue.

So to say the least, when I finished the third grade school year, my parents were notified that I would have to find another school to attend because Harrison School did not want me to return in the fall.

CHAPTER
Four

At this point my parents knew that they had to get me off the northside of Minneapolis. This was 1956, and my parents were very involved in the integration movement in Minneapolis and were both a part of the sit-ins downtown.

In the early fifties in the north and south in America, Negroes were not allowed to eat at lunch counters at drug or department stores. We could sit in a booth but not at the counter with whites (of European descent).

They organized sit-ins, as they were called in those days, that were staged between Sixth and Seventh Street on Nicollet Avenue in Downtown Minneapolis in front of Woolworth's Department Store. The planning and participants in this event were multicultural and people of many religious denominations.

In my life, it was the beginning of my exposure to the civil rights movement. Many of the meetings to discuss strategy took place at my residence, so though my bedroom was down the hall, I could see and hear conversations. It's important to note that my parents had a wide range of friends of many cultures, so I had no idea that there was any difference in people, but I was in for a rude awakening...

My parents made enough friends to enlist in help with their attempt to cross the color line in the South Minneapolis neighborhood they chose to purchase a house in. The dividing line was Forty-Fourth Street, which ran east and west, which meant that the house on Forty-Sixth Street (4609 Fifth Avenue South) was considered block busting. Forty-Sixth Street was two blocks south over the "red line" of Forty-Fourth Street.

My dad used his GI Bill and his three jobs and my mother's job as income, and Mr. Hubert H. Humphrey made sure they got equality.

As was the custom, the neighborhood offered my parents seventy-five thousand dollars as a final offer not to move into a $22,500 house.

We moved into that house in August of 1956 because the school was directly across the street where my parents could keep an eye on me out of the living room window. My parents wanted me to get the best education that their money could buy, and Washburn High School was scholastically number one in the state.

They could have taken the seventy-five thousand dollars and moved somewhere else, but my parents had a dream for me and my four-year-old sister. That dream was the best education that they could provide for us. They understood the value of education because they dropped out of high school early, she at seventeen to get married to her first husband (my father) and my dad to work to financially support his mother and sister. My mother dropped out of Minneapolis Central and returned to vocational school to get her diploma. The second reason for the move was that my attitude needed a different environment.

Prior to the move, I had spent my days playing in my northside neighborhood with my friend Chester Carter. Our kind of playing was burglary. We were kicking people's basement windows in and crawling in and looking around. I didn't want anything, but Chester was a pro at six years old. I didn't know any better; I was a follower.

I remember that August afternoon when my family pulled up and parked the car in front of our new house at 4609 Fifth Avenue South. We were moving the first load of our belongings in the house, and because I was in the way and not very much help, my dad looked out of our living room window and saw that there was a group of kids playing football across the street on the Field Elementary School grounds. He looked at me and said, "Why don't you go outside and play?"

An aspect of my life was about to change, and my cultural innocence would be gone forever as I ran out the door across the street and asked the kids if I could play too.

I joined one of the teams, and I quickly found out that I had much more athletic ability than they did and I had a lot of speed. After I ran for about three or four touchdowns, I heard one of the kids (Tom Lacroix) say, "Look at that jigaboo go!" Pretty soon each time I outran the opposition my teammates would shout, "Go, Jig, go!"

Eventually it got dark, and the streetlights came on and we broke up and called it a day. I left the schoolyard and entered my new home, and my dad saw that I had an upbeat attitude. He asked me, "How do you like your new friends?" My response was "I like them, Daddy, and they liked my touchdowns and gave me a new name." You should have seen my dad's face when I said "Jigaboo"! My ol' man took me back to the schoolyard where Eugene, Tom, and a couple of others were still standing there talking. When I pointed to Eugene who had been the first one to utter the name, Dad then put Eugene and me in the car, and before I knew it we were at the Dairy Queen. My dad bought us both banana splits. Then he asked Eugene to show us where he lived. When we got to Eugene's house, my dad told us to stay in the car, and he proceeded to go to the screen door and knocked. Eugene's father wasn't answering the door. My dad could see him passed out in his lazy chair in the living room with a couple of beer bottles on the floor next to his chair. Dad finally hit the door, and the nail came off the hook. He went in to have a talk with Eugene's father. Dad shook Eugene's father, who woke up startled and wanted to know what my dad was doing in his house. Dad politely introduced himself and explained the fact that we were his new neighbors and that his son Eugene called me Jigaboo. The reply of Eugene's father was "So? Isn't that what he is?" Eugene and I had eaten our banana splits, and with our faces pressed against the screen we saw my dad knock Eugene's much larger father out. As he lay on the floor unconscious, my dad opened the refrigerator, took the ice tray out, and placed the ice in a dish towel. He put the ice on the forehead of Eugene's father while he explained that if that word

15

was used again on those school grounds by anyone, my dad would be back to see him and that he better make sure he had plenty of ice.

The neighbors began contacting realtors, and even though I played with the same kids on the school grounds every day, families began leaving the neighborhood. They were being replaced by colored and mixed-marriage families.

Upon entering Field Elementary School that fall, I noticed that the colored kids came from neighborhoods six and seven blocks away. Fourth grade was my first school experience with the fact that I was different.

The first time I saw Michelle Mercier at school, I was hit by the arrow of Cupid. Michelle was, to me, the prettiest girl in the school and had always been attractive to me because of her dimples. I kept my secret crush to myself until a friend of mine named Raymond Peterson asked me why I was always staring at Michelle. When I confided in him the secret crush, he told me, "You can't like her, she's white!"

Up until that moment I never thought of people as white, so I had no point of reference, and like any scared, confused child of nine years old, I ran home crying. When I got home, it was lunchtime and my father's mother (Guy) was there to make sure I ate my lunch. Because of my hysterical crying condition, Raymond had followed me home. Since he was with me, Guy invited him in to share lunch with me. Guy asked me why I was crying, to which I explained Raymond's "she's white" statement to her. Guy paused for a moment and pushed a white napkin toward Raymond and asked him to place his hand flat on the napkin. Raymond was excited because he anticipated Guy was going to take a pencil and trace around his fingers. Instead Guy asked Raymond to describe the color of the napkin, to which he replied, "White." At that point she asked him what color his hand was on the white napkin. Raymond teared up and got out of his chair and ran out of the house crying. Guy retrieved him and explained to him that there was no such thing as white people and that all that was in his mind. Raymond stopped talking to me, and the Petersons sold their home and moved.

CHAPTER

Five

My parents were what are referred to as civil rights activists and sometimes integrationists. I witnessed my home as the meeting place for many of these organizational meetings. As a child, I saw people of many nationalities sitting in our living room and was so carefully raised to see all people as one people. Because my parents had friends and associates that were diverse, I unconsciously had a multicultural foundation.

By 1960, my home had become a source for intellectual conversations on human rights and change. Even though I was young, I was listening to much of the conversations.

The only discomfort I felt was the fact that when the out-of-towners came to assist my parents with the organization of the March on Washington, especially the members of the Minnesota delegation, they had my bedroom to sleep in while I was relegated to a couch in the basement. My bedroom was the attic portion of the house that had been converted into a two-room study and bedroom, the largest room in the house.

Two of the notables to take over my bedroom were John Lewis and Dick Gregory. At the time, John Lewis was the president of SNCC (Student Nonviolent Coordinating Committee). He discussed voter registration in Mississippi and Selma and other activities.

Both of my parents were involved in freedom rides, voter registration, Selma March, and other events related to the civil rights movement.

I remember Mr. Gregory because he was very famous and a pioneer comedian and a social activist. I sat at the dinner table listening to Mr. Gregory talk and my dad calling him Greg. To me that was especially important to hear my dad on a nickname basis with a man so famous. When Mr. Gregory left, my dad took a picture of us in front of the house, and I remember his white and gray seersucker suit jacket, fancy black dress pants, and spit-shined shoes.

There were wonderful memories of an exposure to so much social history, but as Shakespeare said, "To the victor go the spoils."

In my home behind closed doors, "all was not well in Denmark." My dad was an alcoholic, and his drinking was tearing the bonds of the marriage and family system. My dad's statement of preventing me from being a street angel and home devil had caught up to him. My parents had a sophisticated image that we had to present to the community, but at home my dad was out of control, and his abuse was beyond scary. My dad could consume massive amounts of alcohol and never slur his words or stumble. He did, however, become mean-spirited, and I was his target. This man was working three jobs each day a lot of the time. He worked at the Ford Motor Company in Highland Park putting gasoline tanks in cars on an assembly line. When he left the Ford plant, he would drive home and shower, eat dinner, and drive to a supper club in Golden Valley then known as the Whitehouse, where he waited tables and was a bouncer. At the end of this job, which was usually at 1:00 a.m., he would drive from Golden Valley to a bowling alley in south Minneapolis and clean until 3:00 a.m. This meant he didn't get a lot of rest.

When events would come up like the freedom rides or voter registration in the south, my mother would be the one to attend. He believed in the cause, but someone had to pay the bills while she took a leave of absence from Bell Telephone Company where she worked as a service assistant. He took on the responsibility of two paydays.

With his lack of sleep and my mother being out of town for events, he was not a lot of fun to be around. Whenever my mother was gone, he drank more and became more irritable. It was during this period when my parents changed my name from William Edward Commodore Jr. to William Edward Wynn (my stepfather's last name).

At the end of the sixth-grade school year, my biological father and his third wife had planned to come and get me to have me join them on a trip to California to see Disneyland. Upon their arrival, I stood at the door with my bags packed, ready to go with my school patrol certificate to show them. When they got there, my father looked down at the name on that certificate bearing William Wynn. He threw a tantrum and took off. I wouldn't get to California for another ten years (not with him). My stepfather couldn't deal with the kids in the neighborhood referring to him as Mr. Commodore.

So, I left sixth grade as Billy Commodore and was manufactured into someone named William Wynn. Since my dad (stepfather) had fathered a daughter with my mother when I was five years old, my name change confirmed his feeling of family.

Because of his mood swings on alcohol in his mind, I would fluctuate between being his son to becoming Bill's son under the influence.

One of his greatest frustrations was that when he was being heavy-handed with me, my mom would say, "Bob, you'll kill him!" He would stomp off in a rage, his inability to explode removed from him. It was during the times when my mother was away that he was the most abusive. It was also during this period when he was going in and out of rehabilitation facilities for his abuse of alcohol.

To the outside community, we acted as if we were in harmony, but for me, it was totally confusing trying to live all these contradictions. While the preparations for the delegation for the March on Washington were going on, my personal value diminished to a point where when my parents boarded that plane for the march, I was kneeling by my bed at night asking God not to let them come back alive. Never had I ever been so disappointed in God when they returned to continue our dysfunctional family follies.

Not long after they came back, I had grown so tired of being a scapegoat for their unresolved issues that one night I went into the medicine cabinet and took a bottle of sleeping pills and swallowed a bunch of them. Shortly then after I informed my parents that I had decided to die. My dad yelled at me, "You just go to your room and waste yourself away then." I went to my bedroom, and within minutes I was taken to the bathroom and immersed in a hot bathtub and forced to drink a concoction that included a glass of hot water with red pepper and six raw eggs. I was supposed to regurgitate the contents that they gave me, but I was so stubborn I wouldn't throw up and went to bed. My last prayers were "Goodbye, God." I woke up at about three o'clock the next day riding to Glenwood Hills Hospital in Golden Valley in an ambulance. I spent a week being tested and observed. When the doctor came to my room and asked me how I felt about going home. I refused. The doctor informed my parents that it was best that I stay another week, and my dad was angry. He was worried about his hospitalization insurance and the deductible. At the end of my two-week stay at the hospital, the doctor came in my room and informed me that I seemed to be well rested and would be going back home. Later my mother told me that the doctor told them that I had a case of rebellion. There was no family discussion about what had transpired over the past two weeks. I just went back to my sophomore year at Washburn High School.

It was in the same period that I met Debbie at a career day event, where Twin Cities students attended a workshop where representatives from many companies and corporations gave seminars on their companies' programs and benefits. It was at this conference that Debbie and I exchanged phone numbers. Debbie was a student at St. Paul Central High School and came from a very respectable family. I had been extraordinarily trained in my home to be a gentleman with a girl. I had too much character to go beyond a kiss. Debbie lived in St. Paul. We talked on the phone through the week and got together on Saturdays. Before we could date, I met her parents, and they called and met my mother. Dating began with me riding the bus to St. Paul and returning on the bus later. I would visit with Debbie and Greta, her older sister, in the basement, and they were both down-to-earth, sweet girls. Debbie and I must have been compatible because as innocent as we were, there was no reason for us not to develop into a good relationship. To this day I will never understand what came next. Debbie and I planned to go to a movie in Downtown Minneapolis, so Debbie decided that she would ride the bus from her house and transfer to another bus to my house and we'd catch a bus downtown to attend the movie. Debbie would call me to let me know when she was leaving to come to my house. When I got off the phone, my mother let me know she was going to inspect my Saturday housework duties, which included cleaning, mopping the bathroom and kitchen floors, and cleaning the baseboards also. Knowing that Debbie was on the way, she put a white glove on her hand and began running it over my work and decided to make the decision that was "no date." When Debbie got off the bus at the bus stop, my mother was sitting behind the bus in her car and intercepted Debbie and drove her back home to St. Paul. This act repeated itself three Saturdays in a row, and Debbie informed me that she had to go. Debbie and Greta and I are friends to this day, but my mother had a few power and control issues.

By the time the March on Washington came and my parents both departed, I remember kneeling by my bed the first night they were gone and asked God to do something to keep them from coming back. When my parents came back from the historic march, I was very disappointed in God for sending them back home safely. My dad was so proud of himself for getting Bill Russell's autograph, "To Skip," on a postcard. To be honest, if I had that postcard, it would be very valuable since Bill Russell didn't give autographs.

CHAPTER

Six

My parents may have gone to a historic event by the end of the fall of 1964 but I just couldn't live in that home any longer. I contacted my biological father (William Commodore Sr.) and told him that I wanted to live with him. He broke down and cried when he heard the conditions that I was living under. He had a very small one-bedroom apartment. It was one bedroom with a kitchenette section. The day I moved in with him he took me to the courthouse, and we went to Judge Douglas Amdahl's chambers where he got sole custody of me.

My father took me out and bought me some dress clothes of his taste and began a training and teaching program which, in my words, was a combination of what he learned in the Navy and hardcore street smarts. He took me Downtown Minneapolis at 3:00 a.m., and we sat inside Alice's Plantation Pancake House on Fifth and Hennepin. We sat in a booth where he pointed out the pimps and their "property." We sat until sunup, and when he had schooled me enough, we went home to bed.

The next weekend my father picked up a new 1965 Chevrolet Malibu Super Sport that he had ordered from the factory. We went to the dealership and picked it up, and we drove to Chicago that day.

I must say that my father went first class because we had a room at the Albert Pick Hotel on Congress and Wabash Street.

Once we were in our hotel room, he ordered room service for me, and when my ample meal arrived, he took off into the evening. I got to enjoy a first-class meal and color TV all night.

When I woke up the next morning, he was just coming in, and we got dressed, went to breakfast, and drove to the South Side of Chicago to visit his uncle Chester and his wife in a high-rise apartment building. As we entered the South Side of Chicago community, I remember he made sure I locked my door on my side of his brand-new 1965 automobile. My uncle Chester was by trade a world-renowned political cartoon artist for the *Chicago Defender* newspaper. His works have been preserved online on a site entitled the Commodore Papers by Chesterfield Commodore.

Once I was introduced to Uncle Chester and his wife, they talked while I entertained myself with a caged parakeet with all the feathers around the neck area missing, leaving the tiny pink neck exposed, giving the illusion of the head detached from the body—the strangest sight I ever remember seeing. Chester's wife said she'd spilled bleach on the bird, and this was the result. After about seven hours of visiting, my father announced that we were hitting the road back to Minneapolis, and we said goodbye and left.

My father had zero parenting skills to have known the role of a father, so his approach was to "school me" on life by means of the most bizarre forms of teaching I've ever witnessed. At fifteen years of age I had been so carefully screened from his type of mentality by my stepfather and my mother. I had been very active in my church and was taught to be a gentleman. My exposure to sex and his strict style of instruction was limited to whatever I heard from my male friends who were just as naive as I was.

At fifteen, I was a virgin who really didn't know what intercourse was because I was saving myself for my future wife, but I wasn't sharing this information with anyone else.

Meanwhile, all the way back from Chicago, my father was filling my head with player and pimp mentality and psychology that I had no point of reference for understanding.

Once we arrived back in Minneapolis, my residence was 2201 Fifth Avenue South, an apartment building full of adults, including my grandfather on my mother's side.

My father still worked at Honeywell from 11:00 p.m. to 7:00 a.m. on the third shift as a machinist. This meant that during the day while I was at school, he slept, and when I got back home, I spent my evenings alone five days a week. Saturdays were usually spent watching him drink Johnny Walker Red scotch and him giving me lectures on "being a man."

One particular Saturday morning, he sat in his breakfast nook (he didn't have room for a table, so it was more of a small booth) and told me his life story while he smoked (five packs per day) cigarettes and downed glasses of scotch.

He said that his father was a man named Joseph Edward Aitkin and never said another word about him other than the fact that we were supposed to be Aitkins instead of the out-of-wedlock Commodore name we were using.

He told me of how he had walked in his home and caught his mother in bed with her half brother Herbert Commodore, and he was immediately sent away to Boys Town in Nebraska at the age of thirteen years old. He described the lonely years from thirteen to seventeen when he enlisted in the Navy.

At this point he was so intoxicated that he was crying and screaming in agony and his girlfriend Bessie came running down the hallway from her apartment in despair to see what was wrong. By then it was about 4:00 p.m. and he'd been drinking all day and working himself into such a state of self-pity that he had regressed to the emotions of a primal screaming child.

He was so uncontrollable that Bessie called his mother (Guy) and asked for assistance. By the time my grandmother arrived we had moved him to his bed where he lay on his back kicking his feet and legs in the air like a young child who didn't get what he needed from his mother.

To prove to me that he wasn't lying to me, he made my grandmother admit to her act of incest with her brother, which she did tearfully and that she sent him away to Boys Town. All three of them stood there crying, and I could only look on in total cognitive dissonance.

They put him to bed, and I watched him cry himself to sleep, ending one of the saddest displays of self-pity I'd ever seen. Little did I realize at the time that I would push this event so far back in my subconscious mind that the memory wouldn't return for many years.

So now I was getting on the bus to ride three miles to my high school, where I have made the transition from William Wynn to William Edward Commodore Jr., and everyone who knew me was confused.

From twelve years of age I had established an identity as William Wynn and away from school socially I was known as Skip Wynn. To add insult to injury, although my father had gotten legal custody of me, I was required to visit my mother and stepfather which for a short while I refused to do until my mother went to court and obtained visitation privileges.

My visits back to the home that I had rejected were emotional and tense, to say the least, because my stepfather was a wounded bully, and on my visits he had to reinforce his message of "I will still hurt you."

Another issue was the fact that I was living out of the school district, and my father had a limited amount of time to move our residence closer to the Washburn vicinity.

He found a two-bedroom apartment on Forty-Fourth and Blaisdell, but the racist landlord refused to rent to Negroes. My father tried to fight it with lawyers, but time was running out, and soon I would have to transfer to South High School in a district where we lived.

My father had instructed me not to have anyone in our apartment when he was gone. My friend Curtis Webb had ridden the bus to my place to go to the nearby park and ice skate with me. When Curtis came, I had him stand outside the door in the hallway.

On one of my father's surprise visits on his break from work (sound familiar?) saw Curtis standing outside the door, overreacted, and in a loud fit of rage packed all my belongings and drove Curtis home and drove three blocks and rang my former doorbell and upon the door opening announced that "YOU CAN HAVE YOUR SON BACK."

CHAPTER
Seven

My stepfather answered the doorbell, and when he heard my father say, "You can have your son back," he tried to reason with my father but to no avail. There was no explanation given for such a drastic 180-degree about-face. I brought my clothes and other belongings acquired in the short time that I had lived with my father up to my bedroom. As I moved back in, I realized that I was back unprotected again. My father was gone, and my mother and stepfather felt betrayed by my act of independence and had their way of reinforcing their parental authority over me. My experience living with my father lasted only a few months, but it disrupted my junior year of high school. I fell behind in my grades, so I was not able to compete in track and field, and even though no one on the team said anything, I knew I'd let them down.

My friends saw my experience but never commented on my situation.

In the months that I was gone, my mother and dad had gone from bad to worse, and yet to the community we acted an "as if" public lifestyle because that is what we did.

The fall through the spring I worked as a dishwasher downtown at a department store on Seventh and Nicollet called Woolworth's. The job was only part-time, but it gave me clothes and walking-around money. This job kept me away from the tension and unhappiness in my home. The entire summer of my junior year I worked as a car hop at a drive-in restaurant named Porky's and spent very little time at home, as my parent's marriage was crumbling.

By the fall of my senior year, I was ready to make the best run at graduation I could, and between school and football I was detached from my home environment.

My parents separated, and yet my stepfather came to the house after work and eat dinner and stay until my mother got home from her job at the phone company.

I remember feeling that even though their marriage was coming apart, they tried to maintain their image not just for the neighbors but for my sister and me.

I believe they wanted to get me out of the house before they divorced.

My entire focus was on football, basketball, and the new track season. My senior year was my best year in high school because I wanted to put my personal problems aside and do the best I could. My only regret in sports was that my home life kept me from being a great athlete instead of a very good one.

Up to my senior year, the years were spent in manner that prepared me to enter society as a black male and not just compete but excel. I wasn't taught to be equal; I was taught with the best manners and discipline for all the best reasons.

In reality they prepared me in a brilliant way that I wouldn't realize for many years later because of seventeen years of drama in my parents' behavioral system.

If there was ever a year where I put it all together, it was from the first day of my senior year in September.

I went to my classes and put 100 percent of my attention on learning. My football senior season went well as I was on the junior varsity team as a running back, and football gave me an outlet for anger that was deep inside me. After practice, I made a point to take a bath, eat dinner, and study late into the night.

While some of my friends may have gone to different schools, we spent the weekends socializing on all levels. I joined this church as a member at twelve years of age and was very active for the next six years of my life. We had a new minister named Reverend Johnson that was young and vibrant and focused in a way that changed the social landscape of Minnesota because of his idea of Youth Sunday. One Sunday each month was a designated Youth Day where the youth in the church assume some of the duties such as ushering, the youth choir, and after-church activities.

Reverend Johnson wanted to inform the entire community that St. Peter's Church was open to all members of the community no matter what your cultural background was. To prove his point, he set up a field trip for the youth group in Mound, Minnesota, on Sunday, and that exchange was the revolution of a teenage culture that not just changed the dating standards but music appreciation also.

Our church worship came off well even though the black visitors sat on one side of the church and the white members sat on the other. After the short service we were led to a church basement where there were refreshments served on a table.

Everyone sampled the refreshments, but after obtaining their portions they returned to the other side of the room with their fellow church members.

What you had was whites on one side and blacks on the other side of the room. There was no mixing, and it became uncomfortable when Claudia Brown noticed the forty-five-rpm record player at the end of the refreshment table and reached into her huge purse and pulled out a bunch of forty-fives. We started line dancing to what was referred to as R&B music back then, and the white kids joined in and the segregation was broken. We were invited back on the next Youth Sunday, and the word got out and we visited many white churches. Through the friendships made began a culture that saw the interracial dating and entertainment scene explode in Minnesota.

Because our Youth Sunday expeditions took us to many suburban churches, we fellowshipped with and began developing relationships with kids whose parents weren't happy. Out of this process was born a teenage nightclub called Mr. Lucky's. On Lake Street and Nicollet, this nightclub served pop in mugs and had live music on Friday and Saturday nights and was very popular.

Because of the popularity of Mr. Lucky's, many teenage establishments opened in the suburbs that catered to integrated audiences. Also, out of this culture were the various gangs forming—the Baldies, Greasers, Animals, Northside Poets, etc.

The largest gang by far was an interracial gang called the Suprees. What made this gang stand out from all the others was that not only was it multicultural but it was a mixture of middle-class and wealthy teenagers from the cities and suburbs. The guys became brothers on a spirit level of consciousness and the girls became sisters.

This large group of teenagers had discovered that we could love each other despite what their parents taught.

In this era, Minneapolis would become one of the largest interracial dating and marriage cities in the country. In five short years you had R&B bands and rock bands playing sounds from both. Band members were mixed cultures in many bands, and a new culture arrived in Minnesota. The downside to this movement was the fact that the parents of these teenagers were horrified at what they were witnessing.

Suburban girls dating black males and so on created a counter movement.

With all this going on around me and my own personal unresolved issues, I enjoyed my senior year and graduated in June.

My last memory of Washburn High School was after our commencement ceremony at the school, we all gathered at the Medina Country Club for the senior all-night party. The highlight memory for me was that Barb Erickson walked up and asked me to dance to the Young Rascals' "Good Lovin'."

As I've said earlier, our dances were segregated in junior and senior high school.

One-on-one dancing was preceded by line dancing, where all moves are choreographed and safe.

There was no cheek-to-cheek dancing on an integrated level in our experience in high school. I don't believe to this day that Barb Erickson was attracted to me in any way, but she was a good dancer and wanted a better dancing partner for that dance. For me it was what made her the most beautiful because she was the only Northern European to integrate the dance floor that evening.

CHAPTER

Eight

The very next morning, after the all-night party, I went to the home that I'd been in since I was eight years of age and moved out for the second time. My dad had been living separate from my mother and was renting a one-bedroom upper duplex apartment at 3312 Third Avenue South from a woman named Mrs. Griffin.

My senior year I befriended a man (twenty-one years of age) who came to Washburn from Henry High School named Ron Sayers (yes, Gale Sayers's cousin), and we moved into another place.

This move was supposed to be temporary because Ron and I had enlisted in the United States Air Force and on the 180-day buddy program where we go as a duo to Lackland Air Force Base in Texas. My dad got us jobs at the White House Supper Club in Golden Valley, Minnesota, where I was the dishwasher and Ron stocked the bar. He worked the day shift, and I worked the 4:00 p.m. shift until I finished cleaning up, which could be 1:00 a.m. or later.

To this day I don't know where Ron got the '57 Chevy with bad brakes and no foot pedal on the accelerator. Ron could drive the car and would pick me up at work, and we would begin our adventures.

To be honest I was as "green as grass"—innocent and naive and as cool as I was trying to act. I was a virgin at eighteen years old saving myself for my future wife. Ron was well seasoned at twenty-one and knew the ways of the streets and coached me on my path to manhood. The adventures consisted of riding around Minneapolis and St. Paul just looking at people.

One particular summer day I got up and borrowed my mother's 1960 Ford Falcon, and my cousin Daryl from Cleveland was staying at my mother's house for the summer while my mother got Daryl a position at the phone company where she worked. Daryl and I went to pick up a girl that I was dating, and the three of us went to Lake Calhoun Beach.

This trip would change my life forever. We got to the beach and just walked and watched the people.

Kathy, the girl I was dating, was a girl that I met at fourteen years of age, and our friendship consisted of phone calls or I'd go to her house and sit with her on her front steps and talk.

Our relationship was innocent, and I was a complete gentleman with her. Over the next five years I would call or just visit with her in full view of her family, who only had to look out of the window to monitor our behavior. I liked Kathy and yet never advances beyond sitting on her steps, but I believe Kathy liked me and respected the fact that I never made any advanced such as kissing or even holding her hand. I was a boy who lived six blocks away who showed up every once in a while. Kathy's older sister Patty knew me and knew that I was a "nice boy."

In the years of thirteen to eighteen, I had two other girls that I called just to talk to while I was babysitting to pass the time. I never went beyond phone calls with these girls, but they were comfortable with me because I was safe.

My trip to the beach was the first date with Kathy, and the fact that I had my female cousin with us was respectable.

The three of us walked up and down the beach taking in the scenes when we happened upon a crowd of people witnessing a couple in what would be described as a public display of a man verbally shaming a woman. The girl was one of the girls that I mentioned earlier. Her name was Rozzie. She was standing there allowing herself to be the butt of Jimmy's shaming.

I would make a move that would change my life forever. I interceded and rescued Rozzie, and I gave the car keys to my mother's car to my cousin Daryl and asked her to take Kathy home while I rode in the back seat of a Jeep with Rozzie to her house. I sat on her parents' front porch and talked with her until she was called in for dinner. I remember getting her phone number and walking back to my apartment. It was easy to talk to her because of the talks we had with each other at thirteen years old.

Summer turned to fall, and Ron and I went down to the draft building to take our physicals for the Air Force. We were down at the government building at 6:00 a.m., and at 11:45 a.m., I mentioned to Ron, as we stood in line waiting for the doctors to return to sign out papers, that I had to get my mother's car back to her soon.

This big sergeant walked up to us and said, "Did you hear the baby fellows? He has to get to his mommy. You're on Sam's time now."

Ron said, "Well, Sam's wrong."

That redneck sergeant got in Ron's face and asked, "What did you say, boy?"

Ron answered, "I didn't say nothin'." At that point we both tore our paperwork up and threw it at him.

That sergeant made a big mistake by not finding out our status. We were not draftees and had not taken an oath. Meanwhile, someone alerted our enlistment officer, Sgt. O. G. Smith of Alabama, and he came running down the hall yelling at the redneck sergeant, "You're running my boys off." Ron and I headed for the door as we looked at each other and replied, "Yep, the boys have run off."

By fall I had secured a scholarship to attend Metropolitan State Junior College. Ron attended the Work Opportunity Center to get his GED.

I got a job part-time at Northwestern National Bank wrapping coins in the sub-basement vault. I met two guys that were attending the University of Minnesota, and we are still good friends to this day: Bill Manuel and Wes McGee.

These guys had gone to North High School, and my common connection was my start on the northside. We became instant friends, and I found out that Bill and I shared the same birthdate, May 20. The other aspect that the three of us had in common was that we were juniors and carried our father's names.

We would work four hours and go to our respective schools for the afternoon.

At Metro (as we called it), my strongest course was English, and I had a brilliant female teacher who recognized my talent for creative writing and took a special interest in me and my work. She would give the class an assignment to write on a subject for five hundred words, and I could write on endlessly. We had a great rapport, and I excelled until basketball season started and I tried out.

Bill took me to the gym and tutored me and after all the cuts I made the team, and after about three practices Coach Lievansie called me aside and informed me that he found out that I was skipping three o'clock English to come to practice and that I needed to change my hour of English.

I immediately went to the English teacher's classroom to get my hour changed. I told her of my need to change the hour. She asked me to pull the shade to the door. She then told me that if I agreed to spend the weekend at her house, she would tutor me on the material I missed and changed my class time on Monday. I was naive but not that naive. I pulled the shade up and unlocked the door and walked out. I walked into the student lounge and threw all my books up in the air, asked for a cigarette and light, and got one. As I walked out the door of the lounge into the hall, who should be coming toward me but Coach Lievansie, and in one destructive act of self-destruction, I got kicked off the basketball team and walked away from a junior college scholarship.

Years later, when I analyzed my act, I came up with the fact that I contributed to that teacher's behavior.

I did unconsciously stare at her legs when she sat in front of the class and read to us.

As stupid and naive as I was, I would still have an erection when class was over, and she must have seen me covering myself with my books. When I look back, I would do the same thing today, but fifty years ago there was no such term as *sexual harassment*.

This was the end of my college career, and I will never know what I should have done under the circumstances, but she was a very pretty woman…

In 1967, I enrolled in a course entitled basic electronics at a facility called TCOIC (Twin Cities Opportunities Industrialization Center).

This was an all-Negro nonprofit organization to educate and provide the tools for men and women to be prepared to enter the workforce. I graduated in less than a year and was among the first graduates.

A man named Bill English was a Negro at a company named Control Data Corporation. Mr. English referred me to the plant in Roseville, and I went out and interviewed and was assigned to work in an area called final assembly, where I would put the final stages of their various computers and data display equipment. The pay was $2.15 an hour.

At the time there were only about ten Negroes employed at this plant, and in final assembly there were three others. They were Granville Clay, Phil Hardin, and Walter (Boots) Jones.

I believe that Grant was from down south, Phil was from somewhere east, and Boots was from the northside of Minneapolis.

All three were older than me and were a lot more settled and mature than I was, and they began immediately schooling me regarding the prevailing social climate in Roseville, Minnesota, in particular the plant we were working in. I saw almost total segregation, especially at lunch and break time in the lunchroom.

CHAPTER
Nine

For me, it was an environment that I had spent in the years of junior and senior in Ramsey and Washburn. The conditions and mentality were very similar to that Northern European males seem to have this practice of "giving you shit," which is some sort of initiation to test your boundaries on an emotional level.

I was about nineteen years old at the time and had been dating the girl that I had rescued at the beach that summer day in 1966, and our relationship was getting serious. I bought her an engagement ring, and that was our status.

Almost all the males in final assembly were married, and so I had a lot of taking shit. Sometimes it was racist, but I knew that their system would get me fired if I overreacted to their insults.

My shortcoming was that I was late for work on a regular basis and calling in sick a few times too many to seem stable. There was nothing challenging about the position I had, and because we four Negroes sat in close proximity to each other all day, I learned a great deal about life from these men and got a great deal of guidance from them.

My difficulty was that I was so young and immature and very thin-skinned. I couldn't just let things go and move on. I wore my feelings on my exterior instead of rolling with the insults. Once the Northern European men saw how sensitive I was, the attacks were amplified. I became the butt of many jokes designed to provoke me into being hostile.

This psychological provocation went on daily for over a year, and in the spring of 1968, my fiancée announced her pregnancy to me.

To me, it was no big deal because we were already engaged, so I had no reservations about marrying her and starting a family together. I was so naive about what impact this would have on our families. It was indeed time to break the news to my mom and dad, and I failed miserably in my proclamation and their reaction was less than happy. First of all, my buddy and I just stood in the middle of the living room as I said, "Guess what? You're going to be grandparents." Ron and I started laughing hysterically.

My mom ran from the living room to her bedroom crying, and my dad was beyond angry at my smugness at such a serious time in my life. I didn't have a clue. Later my fiancée called and told me her mother saw her condition as a result of being a tramp instead of a lady. Her father was more than supportive toward her.

The two sets of parents began a whirlwind classical Catholic wedding ceremony in the church with Father Malloy presiding. The parents did all the planning and inviting, and I watched a production unlike anything I've ever seen before.

About a month before the wedding, my fiancée and I were sitting outside her parents' house in the car that we both purchased together, and whatever the main subject was we ended up in an argument that resulted in my calling off the entire event.

She snapped and tried to scratch my eyes out. I intercepted her hands and slapped her on the side of her head. At once I got out of the car and went to her parents' house, rang the doorbell, and announced that the wedding was off.

Her father calmly led me back outside to the front porch and said, "You stop the wedding and you'll never know your child."

With that I knew that the wedding was back on.

His prophetic words would haunt me for the rest of my life: "If you don't marry my daughter, you won't know your child."

I was so young and didn't see the obvious red flags: the fact that I had already been abusive toward her because of her abusiveness and her father's threat.

From this point on the parents took over the entire preparations for what was to become a very elaborate Catholic wedding, middle-class Negro style. The wedding lists where prepared by parents, and the only participation I had was in choosing my groomsmen.

As the time raced by, I was in a fog because I was so very naive that I had no idea what was going on. My life was being controlled by everyone around me. As the days got closer to the May 4 wedding date, the more reluctant I became.

Finally, the night before the wedding, I lay in bed all night looking at the ceiling feeling like I was no longer in charge of my life anymore. I was lying in the bed that I grew up in at my mother's house, and I didn't want to go to the wedding.

At 12:30 p.m., I heard my mother and my best man Ron talking downstairs. They were wondering out loud as to my whereabouts. Finally, Ron came up the stairs to my bedroom, and once he saw me lying on the bed with the covers over my head, he alerted my mother and I had to get ready.

They both saw this as humorous, and I saw it as no laughing matter.

I was dressed at 12:45 p.m. for the 1:00 p.m. wedding, and at the last second my mother handed me two pills and a glass of water and told me to take them. I didn't realize at the time that I was being tranquilized to sleepwalk through the wedding. Ron and I got to the church at 1:00 p.m., and I couldn't believe the amount of people in attendance. I heard later that people were standing outside the doors who couldn't get in because the church was packed.

The tranquilizers my mother gave me were working, and the "I do's" were a blur to me. My next memory was standing next to my bride at the receiving table watching people drop wedding gifts and envelopes while I shook hands and said thank you.

I remember leaving the church, and when my bride and I walked through the doors of the church to go outside, the sun shower rained on the two of us as we headed to the wedding car where Ron was waiting. Some woman exclaimed that the shower was a sign of good luck.

Ron drove us around the neighborhood honking the horn and finally dropped us off at her parents' house. The house was abuzz with women everywhere commenting on the beautiful wedding and describing who was in attendance—Mayor Arthur Naftalin, a close friend of my mother—and who's who of both families and their political connections.

My father-in-law was very wealthy and well-connected in the community.

My mother was quite comfortable, and she and my dad were very solid politically for Negroes.

I sat on the couch still wired on my mother's tranquilizers looking down at the wedding ring on my third finger left hand and asking myself, "What have I gotten myself into this time?"

At 6:00 p.m., we were told that everyone was going to the affair at a private Negro club called the Nacirema, which was American backward. My father-in-law opened the club, and there was food and an open bar all night with a live band. My father-in-law went first class across the board for the occasion.

My bride and I checked into the Curtis Hotel and got into comfortable clothing so that we could relax. The hotel gave us a complementary bottle of champagne, and we had three more bottles and a fifth bottle of Crown Royal in a velvet bag.

I looked down at my royal-blue pajamas (silk) and wedding band and cracked open the champagne and began drinking.

I remember getting into the bed preparing for the honeymoon and woke up at about three or four in the morning to my new bride sitting on a chair next to the bed crying away. I asked her what was wrong, and her reply was "When I tried to get into the bed, you put your hand in my face and pushed me away." I had no memory of this, but what an omen…

CHAPTER

Ten

After two days in the honeymoon suite, we headed for our new home, which was a one-bedroom apartment in South Minneapolis. All our furniture was paid for, and we both had good credit.

That Monday following the honeymoon, we both had to go back to our respective places of employment—she at the *Star Tribune* and myself at Control Data.

After work, I picked her up when she got off, and on the ride home, she informed me of her doctor's advice to stay off her feet. By this she explained that she would not be cooking dinner that evening.

My first thought was that I didn't understand, but I saw her smile as she turned her head away from me at what I perceived as a way of hiding her amusement. As we drove to the apartment, I began to feel like the butt of a joke.

When we got to the apartment, she went to the bedroom and changed into a nightgown. When she came into the living room, I was watching the evening news on television. I got up from the couch and went back to the bedroom and laid myself across the bed in an escalating depression. About ten minutes later, I heard the refrigerator door opening and closing and then the cabinet doors open and close. My thought was that she had changed her mind and was preparing tonight's meal. In the next fifteen minutes that seemed like an eternity, I heard no noise at all.

I got out of the bed and made my walk down the hallway to the living room to inspect the atmosphere.

My new bride was sitting on the couch with a large bowl of ice cream with sliced bananas and whipped cream on the top. My response to this sight was to take the beautiful bowl of desert and smash it into her face with all the bowls contents dripping down her gown, and I walked back down the hallway to the bedroom while I heard her cussing up a storm. She cleaned herself up and headed for the bedroom to be met with a few slaps to her head, and the marriage began dying.

We fought many times in the first apartment.

At one point her brother, who was my age, came over and stated that he didn't want to "whip my ass." I knew that this was a grandstand stunt because I knew I could stand my ground. In about three months my father-in-law informed us that our rent of $125 was too high, so he arranged to have us take over Uncle Clarence's (her great-uncle) apartment for fifty dollars per month.

I saw the move as economic, not realizing that my abusiveness was creating my father-in-law's moves to protect his daughter. In truth I didn't see my own abusive behavior because all the males around me were abusing their women, including my brother-in-law and father-in-law. My wife and I were now living two blocks from her father's house, and with Aunt Winnie, the landlord, living downstairs and my mother-in-law coming over almost every day unannounced, I was feeling as though some of it was an invasion of privacy.

I saw these acts of visitation as an irritant, and I was more abusive as a result.

My wife had a very unhappy pregnancy, and I was too young and self-centered to have any empathy or sympathy for her.

Her father came over at will unannounced and yet never addressed my abusive behavior toward his daughter.

In truth, his son and daughter had told me of his terrorist acts of abuse toward his wife and sons.

In fairness to my father-in-law, I remember him and I in the middle of the lake at his cabin in a boat when he told me of how I didn't want to hit my mate and accidently paralyze her and have the guilt while I wheeled her around in a wheelchair. I didn't get it. Let me say that my father-in-law was my father's Masonic lodge brother and had known my mother and father since before I was born. He was good to me, but I was so emotionally unstable. I was in no way intimidated by him after sixteen years of abuse from my much larger stepfather. I saw him as an adversary and blamed my wife for his lack of respect toward me and my home. I just didn't have a clue.

CHAPTER
Eleven

My employment at Control Data came to an end, and I began my career as a loan collector at First National Bank of Minnesota in Downtown Minneapolis. By day I wore a business suit and carried an attaché case, and after work I was a different personality. My wife and I were the ideal couple outside the home, and I had become an asshole to live with.

I added alcohol to the mix by coming home from the office and having a drink or two before dinner. The alcohol magnified my moods, and my father-in-law was nervous about my behavior toward his daughter.

On Thanksgiving morning, November 28, 1968, I woke up to my wife telling me that it was time to go to deliver the baby. I made a call to her parents and then my mother to inform them of our leaving for the hospital.

As we were going down the steps to the car, my father-in-law pulled up in his station wagon, got out, and proceeded to take his daughter's hand and began leading her to his car. She told him that she wanted to ride with her husband. He was angry, but he got back in his car and followed us all the way to the hospital. It began snowing on the way, and I thought, "Snow on Thanksgiving Day, the morning my baby is to be born."

My mother was already at the hospital when we arrived. My wife went into the labor room, and I sat in the waiting room with my mother and my in-laws. My mother-in-law was all smiles conversing with my mother, and my father-in-law had an attitude. I was happy to be summoned to the labor room where my wife was in a great deal of pain from her labor contractions. I took her hand and tried to comfort her when she began cussing at me and blaming me for her condition and pain that she was experiencing. At one point she grabbed the front of my shirt and pulled the whole front off, buttons and all. I stood there crying, and she ordered me out of the room, so you can imagine the sight of me going back to the waiting room to the parents and my mother with my shirt ripped off and this young inexperienced twenty-year-old crying like a baby in a state of total confusion. They were laughing at the sight, and when I look back, I see the humor in it. I was so young, and all this was so very new to me.

My son was born at about 11:00 a.m., and I named him Robert Leon Commodore.

I did this for two reasons: I did it to honor the man that raised me from two years of age to eighteen years of age.

Was he abusive? Yes, but the instructions, teaching, and love that he gave me far outweighed the abuse.

I survived the abuse, but the support, love, and guidance are with me to this day.

I wanted to make sure that there would not be a William Edward Commodore III to inherit the sins of the father and grandfather.

As I looked at my son through the window where they kept the newborn babies, I realized how my life had changed in just six months. I left the hospital and went back to our apartment and made a few calls to friends and family to share the news of my fatherhood.

I called my biological father, and the first words out of his mouth were "So what's his name?" His question was more accusatory than curiosity, and when I told him my son's name, he nastily hung up the phone on me.

His ignorant, selfish display negatively affected what had been a happy day.

He didn't understand the role my stepfather had played in his absence over an eighteen-year period.

Our home was very loving and peaceful, but the pressure of my father-in-law's constant intervention and controlling ways began to mount up in me.

I began to complain to my wife about her father's constant invasions in our marriage. She was or seemed helpless and had no solution to my problem. I couldn't see that my behavior had created these conditions around me. I was so blind that I couldn't comprehend what was going on around me. The truth was that I had been abusive to the daughter of this family, and they were merely being protective, overprotective if necessary. As they stepped up their protection methods, I brought it to her and held her responsible for their behavior.

It all came to an end when in 1969, I was ranting so loudly that a friend of mine, who happened to be visiting us, heard the voice from the front yard and came up and offered his home to us so that our neighbors wouldn't have to be subject to my noise.

We drove to his home and went in, and he and his family allowed us to discuss our differences in private and left the room. I begin by asking her what she wanted to do. Her response was "I want a divorce."

She had my son sitting next to her, and I blindly, in an insecure act of rage, punched her at least six times in the face.

My friend heard her screams and ran into the living room, and after inspecting the damage to her, he said to me, "I have been trying to be like you, and you were acting just like me." He added, "Why don't you fight me instead?"

He sent me home by myself, and after going home and waiting for about two hours, I called her parents to see if she got there okay.

My father-in-law answered the phone and was crying as he was describing what I had done to his daughter.

He told me that it was over. It was a long weekend, and on Monday at 2:00 p.m., a courier handed me my divorce papers with the judge's rubber stamps and signature. I thought to myself, "This incident happened on Friday, and all of these papers were notarized on Saturday. This man moves swiftly."

I was alone and, like many abusive husbands, became desperate to get their families back.

I had a surrogate family that knew my background because the husband was my father's lodge brother, and both were Freemasons.

I went to them for support because my mother and father and extended family were well-known to them on a church level and had a long history together.

I showed my surrogate mother the papers of divorce. After reading, she replied, "The lawyer is Stanley Roberts," and they recommended that I go and talk to him personally.

The next day I called the lawyer and asked to talk to him. I drove to his home that evening where he greeted me, prayed for me, and we went to church together. After church we went back to his house and I got back to my car and drove off.

In the meantime, my son, who was about six months old at the time, got gravely ill and was in the hospital. My wife called to have me come to the hospital because he was not very responsive. When I walked into the hospital room and called his name out, he came alive and stood up in the bed to see me.

To this day, I believe that when Roz saw this miraculous recovery by my presence and the bond between father and son, it made her think seriously about whether a divorce is what she wanted. The Christian lawyer told her I was a good man, despite her father's forcefulness to rush through a divorce.

After a few days she called to let me know that she had dropped the divorce proceedings and wanted to come home.

Looking back, I understand why all these events went the way that they did. I was a clean-cut, well-educated businessman who was indeed remorseful about my act toward my wife, but I was still a very sick man with no program in place to prevent me from being abusive in the future. In truth I prolonged a horrible marriage for a woman and her family for three more years.

CHAPTER
Twelve

By 1970 I wasn't as abusive, as I had begun a one-year affair with a married woman seven years older than me. This woman was well versed in all the aspects of cheating on her husband.

In my case it was an adventure that became a challenge, and the challenge was exciting.

This woman was a master, and I grew up very quickly in the process of adultery. There were no real problems at home because my attention and energies were elsewhere.

This particular woman was connected politically and very well-off financially. I didn't pay for lunches or motel rooms or dinners. There was no evidence of our ever having been at each occasion.

My cousin had left his job at IBM and relocated with his wife to Southern California and was employed by a computer firm. He was calling off and on and describing Southern California, in particular his San Fernando Valley residence in Van Nuys, California.

By early 1971, I was emotionally drained from "living double," as referenced by singer Lou Rawls's song, and I decided to set up interviews in San Francisco (Northern California) and Los Angeles (Southern California).

I had the regional director of the West Coast NAACP Leonard Carter as my sponsor.

I took a two-week vacation and set up two interviews in Los Angeles and two in San Francisco.

I had an impressive résumé and had worked in both departments at the First National Bank of Minnesota (operations and lending). My interview was at World Headquarters Bank of America.

In my first interview, I realized the value of my Minnesota roots and Scandinavian accent. Almost all people that were raised in

Northern European Scandinavian communities learn to communicate with very understandable diction and enunciation.

Being black from Minnesota and speaking with Minnesota diction subliminally comes across as extraordinary to someone with a New York accent.

Of the five interviews that I had that afternoon, four of the five men were of Italian descent and the last Jewish.

I could hear them in the hallway discussing me, and finally they made me an offer. They wanted to enroll me in the management training program at the Bank of America. They offered to relocate my family and I and employ my wife. I agreed that moment and shook their hands as they said, "Welcome aboard."

I finished my last week of vacation in Los Angeles with my cousin and his wife. They gave me a tour of Hollywood, and that night we went to the Whiskey a Go-Go Nightclub and saw a band called Rufus featuring a singer named Chaka Khan, a tiny girl with a big voice. A trip to the Pacific Ocean and I was sold.

I flew back to Minneapolis and broke the news to my wife, and we began to make plans to move to California. I wanted to get out of my affair, and starting out all over again in a new city seemed right.

My wife and I were excited, but as each day passed my in-laws grew more and more depressed, and my father-in-law was communicating his negative feelings about our move.

In reality he was concerned about his daughter's safety. It was one thing to have us two blocks away and another for us to be 2,800 miles away.

I saw his behavior as controlling, and my mind was made up—we were leaving.

I gave my two weeks' notice at First National Bank of Minnesota, and in my last week of work Bank of America contacted me and informed me that I would be trained at a branch in Berkeley, California.

I told one of the women I was working with, and she said, "Wonderful." When I asked her to describe Berkeley, she said, "You'll see for yourself."

With about four days to go before we leave, every one of her family members is openly depressed and almost antagonistic toward me.

I took all this personally, and with two days to go and everything packed, I packed my bags and left.

I called my mother and asked her to pick my wife up from work that evening.

At the time I didn't understand everyone's depression, but my solution was to leave and follow my dream. Everyone was devastated, and my mind was made up. The night I left, I looked in my rearview mirror at my wife crying and three-year-old son crying *hysterically* as Marvin Gaye is singing "What's Going On" on my tape player.

I drove 2,600 miles to LA nonstop and enjoyed the changing of the landscape as I headed southwest.

Upon arriving in Van Nuys, California, at my cousin's apartment, I crashed on the living room floor and woke up the next day.

My cousin and his wife were living in a singles club called the South Bay Club. Most of the residents were single, but there were a few other married couples living there. I remember the actress Linda Lavin and Ron Liebman sitting at the swimming pool, and I stopped and talked to him a few times. He was a friendly actor, and both would do well in Hollywood in the years to come.

This was 1971, and my cousin and I were among the very few black people in this club. My cousin and I were about as wild and what we thought was psychedelic at the time and acted and engaged in bizarre behavior in front of the crowd around the pool. We were wearing hot pants and on one occasion threw a beautiful redhead into the pool with all her good clothing on. I am getting ahead of myself. My cousin's wife was of Northern European descent (white), and they had what they described as an open marriage. In truth it meant he had a free pass and she had to accept it.

She was the daughter of two highly educated and wealthy parents and with a major in psychology but gave in to her husband's fantasies.

By the time I got to California, he had already moved one of his girlfriends in with them and was rotating the sleeping arrangements with the two women. By this time, I mean every other night at bed-time one woman slept on the couch and the lucky woman got to spend the night in the bedroom with him.

They even tried sleeping three to a bed for a short time, and that ended when the two women's hands met and touched each other on my cousin's "johnson."

This singles club housed many tennis courts and basketball courts, and I made my way to one of the courts and took my twenty-two-year-old Midwestern street game to the court in a few pickup games.

I was enjoying what I thought was a great deal of success in these pickup games, and a photographer took pictures. He developed some of me in action and gave me some. I became quite full of myself until on one occasion I got to the court early and was shooting baskets when a young man about the same age as I walked on the court and we shared the ball shooting.

This young man was about six feet and four inches and very clean cut. He lived in the singles club with his wife and said he was a college student. We decided to go one-on-one, and I couldn't make a basket against his flawless defense and he was hitting jump shots from today what would be three-point range. He was so far out that I stopped guarding him, and in each case, he never missed a shot. After being scorched for three games, I surrendered as I got the point. It was as we were walking off the court when I found out why I was so bad against him. I found out that he was Kenny Booker, the sixth man off the bench for John Wooden's UCLA Bruins National Championship basketball team, the one with a center named Lew Alcindor, later to be known as Kareem Abdul Jabbar.

I stayed at my cousin's place, and he gave me a whirlwind experience of living in Southern California in one week.

We were at parties at homes in Laurel Canyon and enjoying Sunset Strip and what it offered to a twenty-two-year-old green Minnesota kid.

I was astonished, while my cousin and everyone else acted like everything that was dropping my jaw was no big deal. They admonished me for my "new in town" behavior. Between me and you, they were "blowing my mind," as the popular phrase went in the seventies.

CHAPTER
Thirteen

So much for fun, and now I arrived at the Ashby/Shattuck Branch of Bank of America on Monday morning and met with the staff at the branch and received my money for moving expenses. Then I spent the rest of the day finding an apartment.

I settled on a summer sublet apartment at 2500 College, and after moving my belongings indoors, I was content with my furnished new home. I was only a few blocks from work. When I went outside and took a walk. I found out I was living on the campus of the University of California at Berkeley. I got a bite to eat, and believe me when I tell you that Berkeley has a flavor and atmosphere of its own. Years later I found out that Richard Pryor was staying with some people not far from me. He would have been too deep for me.

By day I was in a management training at Bank of America learning the operational systems and loan systems of branch banking. By this I mean that I was trained to perform all the functions of each position in each of the two departments.

With over a thousand branches in California alone, the system was antiquated compared to the main office that I had left in Minneapolis, where every aspect was computerized in 1971 when I left.

After work each day, I would walk around Berkeley, and my soul bathed in the feeling of freedom that Berkeley gave me.

No police anywhere on campus, just campus security.

I called my cousin in LA and told him about this new unbelievable place I had moved to and got him to fly up and take a look, which he did, and he and a gorgeous redhead got off the plane at San Francisco International Airport, where I was waiting to drive them to my Berkeley two-bedroom apartment.

This was a Friday night, and on Saturday, the three of us went sightseeing on Telegraph Avenue, which was the main drag in those days. Berkeley in 1971 was an experience that I don't believe I can accurately describe.

Just about every one of every category of life was there, but in totality the consciousness was on a much higher spiritual level then any place I've been. We enjoyed the afternoon, and they flew back to LA that Sunday. After visiting a friend of mine in what was called the Divisadero District in San Francisco, she took me to Haight Asbury in the city, and I thought Berkeley was deep—Haight Asbury was exactly what you see in the videos, all peace and love. We went over to Fisherman's Warf for a lobster meal with the lobster and other seafood right out of the ocean. Then we visited the Golden Gate Park and drove back over the bridge to Berkeley.

I was having a wonderful time on the weekends, and it distracted me from the purpose of being there.

My wife flew to San Francisco to spend time with me. Her parents were watching our son.

She spent about a week and sat in the apartment while I was at work.

To be honest, I actually remembered her after a few days. By this I believe she came out to see what our status was. Here I could have been more patient and understanding; we would have been living here with our son and with two guaranteed jobs.

To be honest I can look back and see many should-haves, but I wasn't mature and didn't comprehend my responsibility to my wife or son. At this point my son was three years old, and I had quite a bond with him. We were Chico Bobby, and he called me Chico Daddy.

I fell in love with two "ladies" in Los Angeles and the bay area. I was flying by PSA Jet round trip to Los Angeles and back for thirty-three dollars. I would take off on Friday night and leave my car at San Francisco International Airport, board the plane, and in forty-five minutes my cousin would be waiting at the gate and we'd be off on another adventure.

Each weekend was, for me, a different experience, and my cousin went first class in everything he did. He had me loving all of what Los Angeles offered. He and his wife had gone different ways, and he was living the life of a bachelor in Hollywood. On the way to the airport, I looked at my wife and I broke down and cried.

We both realized that I would be living in Berkeley, and she and our son would be living back in Minneapolis.

As soon as I saw her plane leave the ground, I drove back to my apartment and spent the time thinking about what I had done.

By Monday I was back at work at the bank, and as immature and clueless as I was, I didn't realize I'd been described by headquarters in downtown San Francisco as a diamond recommended by the regional director of the West Coast NAACP and a clean-cut man with a wife and son. I had turned into Mr. Hollywood. On two separate occasions I had to call the bank to inform them on Monday morning that I would be at least an hour and a half late for work because I was on my way to the airport in Los Angeles.

I was proving to be a complete fraud, and a flake at that. I had been very mature in my interviews and sold myself, and as each day passed, I was losing more and more ground.

I got a night job in San Francisco as a security guard for some extra money and landed a job at an elementary school where I patrolled the around the school in one-hour intervals, go back to one room, and sit. No reading or radio. Nothing to distract me.

I got a call about a month later from my wife back in Minneapolis, and she had good news for me—she was expecting.

Meanwhile two things happened: In a long conversation with my father back in Minneapolis, I convinced him to get out of Minneapolis and come to the West Coast. The second was that the branch that I was working in gave me a battery of tests based on what I had learned at this point. I passed, but my scores should've been much higher, so they gave me the last check and wished me luck as I cashed it at the teller window.

I had three weeks left on my lease in full when I moved in, so I caught a plane to Minneapolis.

I caught a midnight flight which took three hours to get to Minneapolis, and with the time change no one was going to be happy to pick me up at the airport at 5:30 a.m.

When I walked in what seemed like my old residence, the energy was different. I was too naive and immature to see that everything had changed, and while I was gone, everyone had a plan of protection for my wife. When I say everyone, I mean her family and my mother. I saw everyone as adversaries and behaved very defensively toward everyone. As far as I was concerned, I was "Hollywood cool" and everyone from Minneapolis was considered "farmers." I was so arrogant in my insecurity. My mother was seeing a bass player / cab-driver who offered me an opportunity to learn the taxicab business as an owner of a taxicab and license on a payment per week plan. I told him that I'd think it over.

It was time to go back to Berkeley and my father, who was staying in my apartment.

On the plane back to Berkeley, I kept asking myself if I was making the right decision to go back to Minneapolis and my situation back there, and I kept coming up with a pregnant wife and three-year-old son. When I got back to my apartment in Berkeley, my father was a different look. He had dyed his hair jet black and was speaking a vernacular of a person in their twenties, and he was doing it poorly. He told me of some woman he met one night in San Francisco and details of his one-nighter.

He was attempting to connect with me on what he thought was my level. Somehow, I think he was trying to bond with a son that he hadn't taken the time to get to know.

It was too late. I was headed back to a situation that I had created, and it was indeed time to face the music.

I talked to my cousin in Los Angeles and my father, and both felt that my future was on the West Coast and that to go back to Minneapolis would be a bad decision.

I sat with my father and talked into the night on the many reasons why I should stay with him.

By morning I loaded my belongings into my car and gave him all the keys to the apartment with a little over a month to go on a paid lease. My father had a very disappointed look on his face, but I had a mind of my own, and I was beyond a father-son bonding experience; I had other responsibilities to attend to.

As I pulled out of the driveway onto the street, I looked in the rearview mirror and saw the look on my father's face, the same rearview mirror that I saw my wife and son crying in as I drove off.

Ironically, I would spend the rest of my life looking in the rearview mirror at those three people.

CHAPTER
Fourteen

I drove down Interstate 80 listening to Marvin Gaye's "What's Going On" album on my cassette player in the car. I was driving through Reno when reality began to sink in. I was driving into my own behavior-created environmental condition. I was still without a clue how immature I was. I had left behind an unforgivable mess that touched an unbelievable amount of people. In their minds I was an abuser, deserter, and in general all the horrible things that a wife beater is called, a coward, and I was indeed all that.

To this day I still cannot understand, as horrified as I was when my stepfather abused my mother, why I could not see my own rotten behavior toward my wife and wake up.

As I drove each mile through each state, I know that this was more of a mission than a homecoming to my family. Finally, I was in Des Moines, Iowa, and taking the 35W freeway to Minneapolis.

When I got back to my home in Minneapolis, I knew right away that things had changed. There was a certain amount of unwelcomeness in everyone's attitude toward me.

What is so sad is that instead of being remorseful and humble, I had a new air of disconnect on the basis of what I've experienced and the subliminal threat that was I could always go back to California. I was now arrogant and "Hollywood quick," and to be honest I was a total waste of time for my wife and everyone else. I had the attitude of someone who was just passing the time before I leave again. It was quite obvious that I had come back for the birth of the child only and not the marriage.

I was a disappointment when I left, but coming back, I was a sorry mess.

I was so defensive that I didn't realize the fact that my reputation was mud in my hometown. No one had respect for a woman beater, much less a deserter of family.

CHAPTER

Fifteen

I learned to drive a taxicab in Bloomington, Minnesota, which was a suburb of Minneapolis, and in 1971, there were only two black males driving taxicabs in any of the suburbs.

I was the third to integrate the industry in the suburbs, and it was an experience.

I qualified to drive in the predominately Northern European environment and interact with their customers because I was experienced with working because of my banking background. I was considered safe.

It was culture shock every time I pulled into a driveway. In one instance I pulled into a driveway in Edina and parked in front of the garage door. The window drapes were open, and the woman and her husband looked out. Now the electric garage door opened, and out walked what must have been the husband. He walked over to my window and asked, "Are you our driver?" My response was "I'm the lookout." He was horrified when I told him that the white driver would be there in a few minutes and that while he and his wife were riding to the airport, I was going to rob his house blind.

He was so embarrassed when I asked him what he thought I was doing sitting there in a taxicab. I would show up in a suburb like Burnsville, Minnesota, and ask customers where they were going, and their reply was "We're only going to the airport, but we'll be right back soon." This was even after I loaded four pieces of luggage in the trunk of the cab.

In 1971 Minnesota, I realized that I represented the entire black race everywhere I went, and if I didn't act like I was a credit to my people, there would never be another black person hired. The stereotypes I had to endure were too many to mention, but I had the edge on the customer because I sounded educated, and that equated to sounding "white" and safe. The nine months that I learned the taxicab business inadvertently prepared me for the sales industry later.

As I worked twelve to sixteen hours a day in the cab, my residence changed, and my wife and Mother moved us into the house I grew up in. I soon was going home each night to the horror house I grew up in with all those memories of the dysfunctional, abusive family I belonged to growing up.

I still didn't realize that a trap had been laid for my abusive behavior. Everyone around me was tuned and ready for my future bad behavior.

I had set myself up to lose at whatever I tried to do. My mother had become my landlord with the power to evict me or threaten to (which took me back to the childhood threat of "do what I say or get out"). The worst part was that my mother's boyfriend / con man won my trust with Chicago-style hustle with the taxicab and license that I paid each week for with the promise that at the end of the contract I would own the taxicab and Bloomington operator's license.

He gave me the payment book and stalked me every week with the same question, "You got my bread?" He would ask the dispatcher what my location was, and the entire fleet of his would hunt me down for his pickups. To put it mildly, it was humiliating, but I had to learn to take it as an initiation because I was new to the taxi business. The other drivers teased me with "Got my bread?" and that I was his "baby." Meanwhile, things weren't very well on the home front, and I admit that I was the problem.

I was very negative and verbalizing my self-pity on an hourly basis on my bad days and not showing any form of happiness whatsoever.

Here I had a pregnant wife and a three-year-old son, and I was talking about how great Los Angeles was and how much better it was.

My father-in-law would drop by unannounced and take inventory, and on occasion if I was home at a time that he felt I should be working, he would voice his opinion.

To be quite honest, the marriage was dead at this point, and I believe we both knew that I came back to be with her until the baby was born. It's sad, but I was no longer emotionally attached to the entire picture.

I had become very sick in that I would create an argument for no reason to start my pity party and my poor wife didn't have to utter a single word.

I could go on nonstop for hours and accelerate the insanity all by myself.

My wife, a victim, had to listen to these tirades in fear of what I might do. My daughter was born on December 7, 1971, and this time there were no parents in the waiting room of the hospital.

My deplorable behavior was well-known, and I was receiving only lip service from everyone, but I was so blind I didn't have a clue.

The truth was that an entire large network of people was carefully monitoring my self-destructive behavior and just waiting for me to step out of line.

CHAPTER
Sixteen

One cold night in March, I went home from my shift, and everything was quite different. We went to bed, and upon waking up the next morning, my mother called looking for the rent payment for March. I told my mother that my wife pays the bills and that I'd have to get an explanation, and that was when my mother told me that I was evicted.

I got off the phone enraged over what was going on and verbally went on a tirade for a lot of hours. The next day I got up at 5:30 a.m. and worked hard until about 11:00 p.m. and called my wife to see if she needed anything on my way home. Her reply was that the locks on the house had been changed and the police had been called and were there in the living room. My response was that she had better make some coffee because I was still on my way.

I drove down the freeway at least thirty miles over the speed limit, and when I got to the house, I went in through the garage door. When I got up the steps, I was met by a hysterical woman who hadn't been in this condition on the phone ten minutes earlier. I demanded an explanation, and she seemed to be out of control emotionally. I asked where the police were, and her reply was that they were on their way and would be there soon.

This was a bluff that was intended to make me leave, but in my demented state of mind I was thinking that because nothing had happened that day, there was no reason for these happenings. Now, mind you, I had a three-year-old son sleeping in bed along with a three-month-old daughter.

In a blind, brain-dead panic, I swept my wife up in my arms and carried her down the stairs and through the garage and put her in the taxicab and took off down the street and onto the freeway.

I was yelling, "WHAT IN THE HELL IS GOING ON?"

No response. I said, "Talk to me!" Then I said, "I'LL KILL YOU!" To this day I've heard guys yell those words in the street, but it seemed more of a phrase than a realistic threat. In her panic she jumped from the car, and because I hadn't picked up the speed, she merely skinned her knees but was running around waving her arms yelling, "HE'S GOING TO KILL ME!"

I pulled the car to a stop, put her in, and headed to my friends' house in Brooklyn Park, Minnesota, a nearby suburb.

We got to their apartment, and I went to the living room and my wife went into their bedroom with his wife. Maybe fifteen minutes later, my friends' wife came out of their bedroom to tell me that my wife wanted to stay with them at their place. I told them, "Absolutely not, she's coming with me." When we got back home, I demanded an explanation as to what this was all about.

Her explanation was that my mother and her father had mutually decided that I should move. I was so overwhelmed by all the emotion that I asked her if I could leave in the morning and after I found lodging if I could come back and get my belongings.

She said yes.

The next morning at the suggestion of my mother's boyfriend, I moved onto the Mendota Heights Motel, another suburb.

When I returned to pick up my belongings, I found that all the locks were changed and I called the police.

When the police arrived, I asked if I could break a window and let myself in. After checking my identification, the officer told me I could gain entrance. I went in, and when I came out to load my cab with my belongings, they allowed me to make three trips to the car. After everything was in the trunk, they informed me that there was a warrant for my arrest and proceeded to put me in the squad car.

I spent the night in jail, and every one of the officers asked me if I was related to my uncle who was on the force. My reply was affirmative, and they'd just smile.

The next morning, I came out of my cell and was escorted to a courtroom, where a judge told me that I had been accused of hitting my wife fifty-two times and kicking her over thirty times over an argument over butter. Everyone in the courtroom laughed as he asked me how I pled.

I told the judge that I was guilty of striking her in the past, but these charges were false. The judge gave me a 180-day sentence if I committed any future offense against my wife and told me that I was free to go.

As soon as I walked out into the hallway to leave, I was intercepted by Lt. Russell Krueger, homicide division.

He took me upstairs and told me that he was trying to get to the courtroom to talk to the judge about my attempted homicide against my wife. Once again, I was asked if I was related to my uncle on the force.

Once I answered affirmative, he told me that he knew my uncle and father well and asked me my story.

I told him the truth in detail, even the "I'll kill you!" that I never meant.

I told them I wasn't capable of killing anyone.

He must've believed me because he had seen my wife that morning when she came into his department to place the complaint accompanied be my mother, her father, and my seventeen-year-old brother-in-law.

Lieutenant Krueger told me that my wife didn't want to sign the complaint, but that my mother said that if she didn't sign the paperwork, she would have me committed to a psych ward. My father-in-law and brother-in-law threatened to kill me, and then he told me something that I'll remember for the rest of my life.

He told me that he couldn't protect me from my father-in-law because of his connection in the community, wealth, and last but not least, his Masonic standing. I looked at the cross with Jesus around his neck in full view for all to see and understood. His final advice was for me to *leave town*.

On my ride back to my motel room, I thought about the fact that when a high-ranking member of the police department advises you to leave town because the law cannot protect you, then it's time to go.

As a twenty-three-year-old young man, I was stunned.

I spent the next week working in the taxicab.

CHAPTER

Seventeen

One Saturday morning, I decided to get a haircut in the city. I took the 35W freeway to the Forty-Sixth Street North exit, and upon making a right turn, someone's bumper collided with my rear bumper. In those days, the bumpers were made of steel.

Upon looking in my rearview mirror, I discovered my father-in-law was ramming my taxicab with his station wagon. He rammed me three more blocks down Fourth Avenue until I got to Forty-Third Street and parked at Eddie's Barbershop.

My father-in-law parked behind me and came up to my driver's window and out of his mouth came the words, "You're finished in this town! You have no family, friends, and soon we're going to take that taxicab away from you." Next, he said, "You accused me of f——g my daughter, and we're going to get you."

That's when I got out of the car and stepped toward him and reminded him of the night a month earlier when I went to his house at 2:00 a.m. and woke him and his wife up.

They sat in their bathrobes in the living room when I informed them that my wife stated the power that they had over my marriage and that he had an incestuous relationship with her, and I had already confronted them about his physical abuse toward her in the past. So, my question was, "Is this true?"

My mother-in-law looked at the floor, and my father-in-law never uttered a word except "good night" while he walked me to the door. As a matter of fact, this matter was never resolved. So, when he referred to that episode, he twisted the incident.

As young and dumb as I was, I didn't connect my confrontation of my father-in-law to the death threats that I was receiving from my brother-in-law in the evenings when I was at the motel.

He was screaming, "We're going to kill you!"

Each evening I recorded his death threats on my cassette recorder and dated them.

After I reminded my father-in-law that he got his facts wrong and that his daughter was the one who gave me the information on his acts of incest, he wanted to assault me, but he knew that I had already shown him on a few different occasions that I was not one bit afraid of him. I had lived with a stepfather who stood 6' 1 1/2" and 190 pounds and took his abuse, and no fat five-foot-seven fifty-year-old man is going to scare me.

He walked off angrily to his car, and I went into the packed barbershop.

Everyone in the shop had seen the scene from the time I turned the corner and parked.

As I waited for a chair in the order I came in, I explained to my barber Eddie what the scene was about, and everyone in the shop knew who my father-in-law was.

Eddie was kind enough to let me bypass the rest of the customers and told me to get in his chair so that I could get out of there.

His intuition was, as they say, spot-on. About fifteen minutes after, my father-in-law returned with his seventeen-year-old son. In a dramatic scene he announced to everyone in the shop that he had a thousand dollars in his pocket to cover the damage to the shop while the two of them tore me up. As soon as he said it, he walked over to the sink and took one of Eddie's hot facial towels and slapped me across the face while his son threw the contents of the bottle of the orange Nesbit pop on my face and the front of the apron I was wearing.

Eddie whispered in my ear, "You want me to call the police?"

I said yes and left the barbershop and went next door to the cleaners.

A friend named Twilah was working and asked her if I could lock her door and use the phone. She said yes, and I called a friend of mine in St. Paul where my stepfather lived. She contacted him by phone and told him of my situation. When I got off the phone, I saw my father-in-law standing outside with both of his sons. It wasn't long before the five squads arrived along with my stepfather and the son of a woman that he was living with who was about six feet and six inches and well over two hundred pounds.

The police interviewed the witnesses in the shop, and they confirmed the assault. My dad told me that he was proud of me for not retaliating and making things worse.

He told me that my father-in-law had said, "I'm going to get that yellow MF."

My dad told me that he told my father-in-law that if harm came to one hair of his son's head, he would die and go to hell with him.

I told him of my tapes and the death threats, and the next morning we were sitting in Judge Susan Sedgewick's chambers.

She looked at the police reports, and after listening to the tapes, she told us that my father-in-law and one son would be arrested and jailed during the dinner hour.

That evening the police interrupted their meal and took them to jail, and my father-in-law was yelling about suing me for a hundred thousand dollars.

I went back to my hotel room, and my mind was blown.

The next day my mother called me to tell me that my cousin Phillip was in town from Los Angeles and was staying at his mother's house and I should go see him.

I was so very young and naive that I didn't comprehend the network of people involved in my departure. I called my cousin on the phone and went over to my aunt's house where he was staying. After I told him my story, we decided it was time to go.

My court date for my father-in-law's case was slated for some time in July, which was a couple of weeks away, and my mother was demanding that I attend so that they could get their due. Meanwhile, I went to my mother's boyfriend whom I had been paying weekly for the taxicab and license. That's when I found out that I had paid off the balance, and without informing me of his move, he refinanced the loan at the bank and got a cash advance.

He agreed to send me a hundred dollars per week out to Los Angeles, but to this day I never got a dime.

I went back to my motel and packed what I could fly with and left all my worldly possessions in that room at the Mendota Heights Motel. The next day my cousin and I went to the airport in my taxicab, and I parked it and walked away from a three-thousand-dollar Chicago hustle. Even my mother's boyfriend got me. Phillip and I drank champagne on the flight back to Los Angeles, and three hours later I was back in Van Nuys, California, in the San Fernando Valley.

CHAPTER
Eighteen

Phillip lived in a very nice apartment complex and shared it with an attractive Italian woman named Phyllis Scutella from Johnstown, Pennsylvania.

Phyllis was one of the sweetest women I ever met and was honest. For about two weeks, I sat in their living room with a pair of headphones on my head listening to the Chi-Lites album *The Coldest Days of My Life*.

I was trying to put my life into perspective.

I had lost a life with a wife and two children, and my reputation was toast in Minneapolis.

I knew that I had to start a new life for myself, and yet I was so self-absorbed that I was grieving the loss of a family that I never really knew. After about the two-week mark of watching me in my self-pity mindset, my cousin came in the apartment, and he and a group of people he brought home with him were having drinks and heading to Hollywood.

I was immersed in so much self-pity that I passed on the offer of going with them. My cousin then requested that at least I could have a drink with him and his guests.

I requested scotch on the rocks, and he gave me a double shot. I was not informed that he had dropped LSD in the drink along with the ice cubes. Everyone saw the move, and they said they were leaving as they laughed on the way out the door. The laugh was on me in a few minutes as my grieving the Chi-Lites turned into a surprise acid trip—as if my mind wasn't already blown. I cannot begin to describe the events of my trip except to say I ran out of the apartment, locked it and knocked on the door across the hall.

Let me say that this sight of a man named Joey answered the door, and whatever I said to him he calmly walked me out of the complex and onto Sepulveda Boulevard. We walked as I talked to him, and we stopped at his hot dog stand. He fed me three hot dogs and a large glass of milk. After I finished, he had me walk up and down the boulevard until the sun came up, and he walked me to the door where I thanked him as we both went back into our respective apartments.

When I sat down in the apartment, I looked at the walls for at least another four hours before I fell asleep. Welcome to Los Angeles, California.

Joey never asked me any questions about that night, but God bless him.

CHAPTER
Nineteen

It was time to go to work, and at my cousin's suggestion, I took on a new career in the automobile sales business.

He was working at a dealership in Burbank, which was east of us about fifteen minutes away.

He was the number one salesman based on his having been salesman of the month in June.

This dealership (Golden State Chrysler / Plymouth) was what was referred to as the fast track because of the caliber of the sales force. I wasn't ready for this, so they sent my green ass to Highland Park, California, where I could learn to sell.

I was so green, but I had an impressive résumé.

Vic was the general manager of the dealership, and he was five feet and ten inches tall but strong and stocky at sixty years of age. Vic was a former all-American fullback for the Army's football team in the fifties. Vic never smiled, but he liked me. He called me Schvartze—never my name, just Schvartze.

In Hebrew it means black. At the time I didn't know it and just followed directions. He called me into his office one day, and he asked me where I was from.

When I said Minneapolis, Minnesota, he wanted to know where that was. He was from the East Coast and wanted to know if everyone sounded like me. On another occasion, he sent me to the bank in his Rolls Royce with a bag and a deposit slip folded. When I returned to his office with his deposit slip, he threw it to me and asked me to look at it. I opened it up to see that it had been a cash deposit for $159,000. I immediately got a mixture of fear and anger that he would tempt me with that kind of money in cash. I told him of my anger at being set up and how I could have left town. He interrupted me, laughing, and informed me that I had been followed the entire time. He told me to come in the next day before 3:00 p.m. because he wanted me to meet someone. The next day I got to the dealership and waited, and at 2:58 p.m., Sugar Ray Robinson walked through the door.

Mr. Robinson had a presence like no one I've ever seen. In 1967, Muhammed Ali spoke at the University of Minnesota at Northrup Auditorium.

His topic was entitled "The Intoxication of Life."

After his speech, he came down onto the main floor, and a few of us in the audience got to go up and speak to him. I was about two feet away from him, and I was frozen in awe at such a perfect heavyweight champion.

My mother got his autographed picture for me. She was the administrative secretary for the African American studies department and did the booking for him.

Mr. Robinson had a presence greater than Ali.

He was a humble, beautiful human being, soft-spoken and gentlemanly in every way. Without a doubt he was the most impressive person I've known. Of my relationship with Mr. Robinson, I will say that in my opinion, he was an honest man. We had two things in common: birthdays in May and our abuse of women.

Beyond that I won't say anymore out of respect to the "original."

For Vic to introduce me to Mr. Robinson was a demonstration of faith.

CHAPTER

Twenty

I was still a green, inexperienced car salesman, and in an era of Los Angeles auto sales, I was just getting started. Don Woolbright was an experienced salesman who helped me sell my first car to Percy Richardson.

I don't know about anyone else, but I remember my first customer.

Percy was a Southern homegrown Negro who talked slow. I greeted him and let him look at used cars.

It was kind of like a kid fishing for the first time and getting bite after bite and not knowing what to do and someone has to take your fishing pole and reel in the fish.

Don Woolbright took over, and the three of us took the car for a demonstration ride. Don changed his accent to sound like a Southern hillbilly and found common ground with Percy. It was ninety degrees that afternoon, and we were riding around with the windows up when Percy asked if the car has "air."

"Of course," said Don and pointed to the word *Air* on the temperature section. Don turned on what was obviously heat and said that we needed Freon but no problem.

When we got back to the dealership and wrote him up, I found out that not only did they take what would have been enough cash to cover the retail sale of the car, but they also used it as a down payment and financed the balance and Percy for an additional payment of five hundred dollars in two weeks. I had earned my first money on half the deal.

In about a month they transferred me to Golden State Chrysler / Plymouth in beautiful downtown Burbank, California.

To put it mildly, this dealership was more than a fast track; it was a circus. By this I mean that they had a sales force of about twenty people, and they were seasoned professionals. Some of them were professional stuntmen from Warner Brothers Studios down the street, and every now and then they would stage "fights" on the showroom floor to attract the attention of the customers. When the lot was full of customers, they would go into their act, and it looked as real as in the movies and shocked the customers. This was done to loosen the customers up when they realized that the staged event was for their entertainment. The salesmen in this dealership were seasoned, experienced veterans that knew how to sell cars.

My cousin Phillip was the top salesman in the dealership when I got there. He was driving a loaded (full of appointments) 1973 Plymouth Grand Fury sedan that was a beautiful two-toned gray-and-black car. We all were given what were called demonstrators or cars to use for transportation. My cousin drove the best car because he had been the top salesman in the dealership for a number of months.

In comparison, I was considered a green pea or beginner in the business, and when you start out, you are treated in a manner that is sort of like an initiation of sorts in that you earn respect through your ability to sell. The point is that I had absolutely no background in sales of any kind whatsoever. No one really teaches you how to sell; you learn as you go, and you work on commission with a minimum wage salary. By numbers you choose the customer in order as your turn comes, and when a customer walks on the lot, it's called an up, which means it's your turn or "You're up." At that point, you greet the customer, and from there everything begins. I had been dealing with the public my entire life, but this was a whole different arena for me, and I was scared. I was taught to help the customer select the auto of his choice, take a demonstration ride with the customer, and upon return to the dealership, if this was the automobile that they wanted to buy, take them into your office where you qualified the customers method of purchase.

Once you determined the method of payment, you took a coversheet out and wrote the pertinent information about the car and customer's information.

If it was a credit buy, you filled out a credit application while asking the customer their information as you go down the form. If there's a trade-in involved in the sale, you collect the information on the trade-in.

If it's a cash purchase, you write up the customer's offer and get a signature that shows the customer's intent to buy the car today.

In each case, once the offer is made, you take the paperwork to a "closer" (one who takes the customer the rest of the way to completion of the sale).

Sounds simple on paper, but the *art of the sale* is very complex and comes with experience learned through time. I was not very good for about five months. I was on the bottom of the list of salesmen each month, and because of my cousin's insistence and maybe credentials, they continued to keep me employed.

I struggled until a woman that I will never forget changed my life—Dona K. Williams.

I had been living with my cousin and his girlfriend Phyllis in Van Nuys, California, when I moved out and lived with a woman I'd met, and in a very short time later I moved out and moved in with my cousin Phillip's other girlfriend living in San Gabriel, California.

Phillip moved me in with him and Dona. Dona was an Iowan girl who had a soft spiritual presence and seemed quiet.

What we had in common was that she was a Taurus just like myself. Phillip had at least four or five girlfriends in different cities in Los Angeles County, and all the women seemed to go with his "program."

I spent many nights with Dona while Phillip made his rounds. My bed was the couch, and it was good enough for me.

Dona worked for David Wolper Productions in Los Angeles and was indeed very intelligent, and I enjoyed spending hours talking with her. I wasn't selling many cars at work, and my confidence level wasn't very high, yet she gave me encouragement to keep trying. I was so pitiful that two days before Christmas, the sales force at work took up a collection to give me spending money for a trip to San Diego for Christmas that Phillip had set up for me without consulting me about it.

It seems that Dona had arranged for Phillip to meet her family who lived in San Diego.

Phillip had bragged to the other salesmen that he was sending his "babysitter" to substitute for him while he spent Christmas at home with Phyllis in Van Nuys. To the people at the dealership, I looked like not only a poor excuse for a salesman but a dumb subordinate to my cousin. Dona and I packed her 1966 Ford Mustang, and she took the wheel for a drive to San Diego and I looked for a station on the radio. I don't recall our conversation, but at one point she took my hand and held it the rest of the trip.

When we arrived at her family's house in San Diego, we went inside, and my role became the boyfriend that she had told them about. We ate dinner as a group and sat in the living room and talked until bedtime, and they said good night to us and retired to their bedrooms. Dona took my hand and led me to our bedroom, and the next morning we had breakfast with the rest of the family.

It was a very nice quiet Christmas and the beginning of a change in my personal life. The next day we packed her car and hugged everyone, and we got on the freeway toward home.

Let me stop and say that San Diego was and is the most beautiful place I've ever seen, with the ocean and temperature in the mid-seventies every day of the year.

CHAPTER
Twenty-One

Dona and I arrived back at home and unpacked the car and went in, and we were now a couple.

We were a contrast in my mind because I had never been with a blonde.

We were the same age, but she was miles ahead of me in maturity, but I was learning. One night I got home from work very despondent from another day with no sales.

After listening to my disappointment, Dona left the room and came back with a blank piece of notebook paper and a pen and asked me to list my desires in number of importance. I wrote number one: top salesman for the month of January. Number two was three thousand dollars in earnings. Number three was Phillip's demo.

I can only tell you that she took my list and Scotch Taped it to the upper left corner of the bathroom mirror and told me that it didn't make any difference whether I looked at what I'd written or not, that when I stood at the sink in the morning, I would bring these things to pass.

From the first workday in January, I went back to the dealership a different salesman. I began to sell cars like hot cakes and had a new-found confidence that none of us, including myself, had ever seen.

Halfway through the month, I believe my cousin felt threatened by my progress and said to me in front of the other salesmen, "I've outrun everyone in the sales force who raced me at fifty dollars apiece, so I might as well take your fifty dollars too."

At that everyone in the dealership got wind of the pending race and the general managers, office staff, lot boys, and mechanics all turned out to witness the *great race*. Mind you, this was on Olive Avenue in Burbank, which was a very busy street, and next door to us was Burbank Ford, a competitor. We marked out a hundred yards on the blacktop in front of the dealership where everyone came out to see what the assembly was about.

My cousin grossly underestimated my speed, as I was a sprinter at Washburn High School and was varsity as a sophomore.

Phillip was at best on the B squad at Central High School in the same city and was about to be embarrassed.

We kicked our dress shoes off and took our marks at the starting line, and we looked to salesman Bob Maurice at the hundred-yard mark of the finish line to bring his arm down to signal the start of the race.

When Bob's arm came down, we were off, and at the fifty-yard mark, I shifted into second gear and left Phillip. At the seventy-five-yard mark, he faked a hamstring injury and quit, and to this day I have never collected my fifty dollars, but I made my point.

At the three-quarter mark of the sales month, I was leading the pack of salesmen and gaining momentum.

This particular night Dona told that we were going to entertain guests for the evening, her best girlfriend, Loretta McLemore, and her date, Al Cook. I looked forward to it because since becoming a couple, we really hadn't entertained anyone. Loretta was the younger sister of a singer for a singing group known as the Fifth Dimension with a worldwide reputation. Her brother's name was Lamont McLemore.

Loretta was a beautiful woman, and Al was handsome. The four of us sat on the floor of the living room, and it was a very pleasant exchange. Al and I connected in that he and I shared Taurus signs. Just when we were all enjoying each other, my cousin came through the back door unannounced in a drunken state.

He still thought that he was the head of the house and was at his arrogant best.

Phil sat down on the floor with us, and the conversation turned to what he did for a living, which was sell cars. Al stated the he might be in the market to buy a car soon and that he'd like Phil's business card.

Phil began to qualify him right there in the living room by asking Al what kind of car he was looking for. Al replied that he was looking for a used Volkswagen. At that point Phil stated, "You can deal with my cousin here because he takes care of the light work." Al repeated, "Light work, huh?" He then turned and asked me for my card and asked if I could take care of his "light work." At that point Phil got up, went to the kitchen, and came back with a small glass of scotch and in one motion threw the beverage in Al's face.

To say that we were all stunned is an understatement.

I got up and got Al a dish towel to wipe his face with. Al was so angry that smoke was coming out his ears, but he kept his composure. I asked him to step outside in the backyard with me, and I then explained to him that I was on his side and that whatever he wanted to do about this situation I was watching his back because my cousin was wrong. We went back inside, and Al asked Loretta if they could go. She said yes, and Al gave me his phone number.

I called Al about a week later, and I found out that he was an accomplished actor and was along with many leading black actors in Hollywood combining to bring to the screen an adaptation of a novel written by Samuel Greenlee called *The Spook Who Sat by the Door*. The movie was about one of the first black FBI agents recruited to the bureau in 1962. This movie was directed by Ivan Dixon, and the novel's author cowrote the screenplay.

When he was mentioning people like Lincoln Kilpatrick and Ivan Dixon among others that were involved in this project, I realized by his tone that this was an important movie for black people. In the seventies, there were many movies with black actors made that were labeled black exploitation movies because the movies were delivering an image that was deemed counterproductive by some members of black society. We were depicted as drug dealers, pimps, criminals, and black superheroes. These roles gave black actors (men and women) acting roles to pay their bills.

I met Al in 1972 and only talked to him a few more times. From what he told me, he took Loretta home, but on the way, his displaced anger and humiliation from Phillip was taken out on her for taking him to such an environment.

The truth was that Dona and Loretta had a very spiritual connection and that when Loretta was gravely ill, Dona used some of her metaphysical abilities to bring a healing to Loretta and that Loretta thought she was bringing him to a peaceful environment.

I guess that first date was their last. Al was a dedicated Brooklyn, New Yorker who wanted no nonsense.

I saw the movie in 1973 at the Pantages Theater, and it affected me like no other movie has because of many aspects within it. I could identify with the experience of being in predominately white environments and being one of only a few.

The Spook Who Sat by the Door was in theaters only about a week in Los Angeles and was removed from the theater's period.

I believe that the nature of the movie was revolutionary and gave black people too much information regarding infiltration and assimilation for revolutionary purposes. I followed Al Cook for years to see his roles in Hollywood, and I believe he was blackballed for acting in that movie. He got small cameos but never a lead role.

I believe that those who collaborated to make this movie were trying to make a difference.

Back at the dealership, I was selling cars like hot cakes, and I did so because of my state of mind.

After Al and Loretta left, Dona took Phillip back to the bedroom, and whatever she said to him, he came out with a few belongings he had and told me he'd see me at work the next day. So far, he lost the race; the "babysitter" took his woman, and at the three-quarter mark of the sales contest, Phillip was so far behind me in sales he quit the dealership and went to sell Mazdas. The "babysitter" was the top salesman in the dealership and was driving Phil's old demo, the Grand Coupe.

I accomplished all the goals that I had on the list that I had taped to the mirror. Dona taught me a lot of esoteric information. One of the most important books that she gave me was called *The Game of Life and How to Play It* by Florence Shinn. Dona was one of the most beautiful human beings that I've ever met and a pure soul if there ever was one. She even cosigned for my financing a 1966 Mustang, and everyone at the dealership sensed my departure wasn't far away. The general manager Bob Walker told me that I was buying an escape machine "now that I was rich."

Dona sat down with me and sensed that I wasn't in love with her and that she was with me and was frustrated. As a result Loretta called me at work and asked me my feelings for Dona and told me that she didn't want Dona to be hurt.

CHAPTER

Twenty-Two

I moved back to Van Nuys on the same Sepulveda block that Phil and Phyllis lived on and rented a one-bedroom furnished apartment. Dona bought me a set of dishes and silverware, and I had my own space. I changed dealerships, and by this, I mean that Jerry Cutter owned many dealerships in Los Angeles County, and I left Burbank and began anew in North Hollywood.

This dealership was called Universal Ford on 5545 Lankershim Boulevard. I was on the used car lot, and I came there with a reputation of being a great salesman.

To be honest, all that I did was go to work and go back home and listen to jazz music. The sales force on the used car lot was strong in that they were seasoned professionals.

The used cars that were in inventory were top-notch and reasonable in price. I was laying out the keys for the used cars, and an old man came up and asked to keep me company.

I had no problem with his company. He introduced himself as Mr. Jackie Coogan and asked me if I knew of him.

I told him, "Of course I know you." Mr. Coogan (Uncle Fester from the Adams family) and I talked every morning as I laid the keys out.

He told me his story. He had been a millionaire seven different times. He told me of being taken advantage of as a child star and how a law to protect child stars was put into place for protection.

Mr. Coogan was one of the nicest, kindest people I've ever met in my life because he shared his story with me.

I sold a lot of cars in the dealership, and because I ate, slept, and dreamed the automobile business, I was able to put a lot of my earnings in a savings account. The salesmen that I worked with were great at selling cars, and we had a lot of respect for each other's ability. My greatest quality was my Minnesota Scandinavian accent. Many of my customers were phone calls that answered newspaper ads on cars we were selling. The customer would talk to me on the phone, and we would agree to meet at the dealership and upon meeting me would subconsciously try to match my phone voice with my black skin.

This always gave me a psychological edge over the customer. On one occasion, I sold four cars earlier in the day, and Zino and Betty Delmonte walked on the lot at about 7:30 p.m. To cut through the chase, I ultimately sold them five cars and wrote up the sale, and almost all the sales force and management remained at the dealership because they didn't believe that the sales would go through. We kept the dealership open until a little past 1:00 a.m. when all the paperwork was completed. People were making side bets on whether the financing would go through.

The next morning when I went to work, I was notified that all nine sales were clearing the financing. I had sold nine cars in one day and five to a family of four.

Mr. Coogan told me that I had a special quality that made me a magnet for customers. I was selling so many cars until I was almost getting sick of selling.

Mr. and Mrs. Willie Johnson came on the lot one evening, and I sold them a 1972 Ford Pinto three-door runabout. Willie wanted to take the car to his home in Pacoima, California, to get approval from his wife and kids.

I drove the car to their house, and when his daughters came out of the house, I saw one named Wilma and asked Willie and his wife, Hazel, if I could ask their daughter out on a date. Wilma Jean Johnson and I began dating.

I was on a roll selling cars and banking almost all my money, and I literally had two or three commission checks sitting uncashed in my dresser drawer.

My cousin Phil had come to the dealership and was selling on a different part of the dealership, but we were both interested in the upcoming Watergate trials on television, and I wanted to watch them each day.

I could only watch Watergate if I was at home, so I quit my job, and Phil and I played golf in the morning and spent the rest of that day watching President Nixon and his people testifying and all getting exposed.

After Watergate was over, I was getting low in funds from taking Wilma out every night, and I realized that it was time to go back to work. Willie and Hazel and family were in the apartment-cleaning business, and when I showed an interest, they taught Phil and I the ropes of the business and got us started with a few buildings.

We had to have a company name, so that was how Trucom Apartment Cleaning Service was born. Tru from Phil's last name and Com from my last name Commodore. We had state-of-the-art business cards made, and we got the yellow pages and began cold-calling major companies like Coldwell Banker, Griffen Von Dyal, etc. and asked for the person who handled apartment cleaning services.

Once we got those people on the phone, we asked if they had heard of our service. We then made an appointment for our management team to come out and discuss prices.

We let them know that our prices were competitive.

Phil and I would put our business attire on and go in and negotiate our prices. Soon we had access to fifty-eight apartment buildings in the Los Angeles area and knew we needed a business manager. I chose Zino and Betty Delmonte to run our affairs because we had expanded our base to rapidly.

We had a two-man operation and had to do all the cleaning.

We were doing quite well when Phil began making business decisions without consulting me, and in one case he hired three people he had befriended and told them that they would make five dollars per hour. He also wanted to expand the business to include rug shampooing.

Our operating vehicle was my 1966 Mustang, and to fill it with our cleaning tools and supplies was getting to be too much. Phil wanted to purchase brand-new vans that we could have for recreational purposes on the weekends.

This was too much for me, but the straw that broke the camel's back came one night when Phil, Phyllis, Wilma, and I went to dinner. Phil had too much to drink, and in an intoxicated state, he stood on the top of the hood of my car and, with Wilma and I sitting inside the car, took his penis out and urinated on my windshield. By then Wilma and I were living together in a two-bedroom apartment in Panorama City, California, and Wilma lost a lot of respect for me for letting my cousin show so much contempt for me. By the following Monday, I took my name off the "doing business as" and gave him the whole business.

I then applied for a job with Crocker National Bank and qualified for their management training program.

CHAPTER
Twenty-Three

O n one occasion, my father, who was by then a truck driver, upon coming to a city in California, came to visit. Phil and one of his many girlfriends came by, and my father was sitting at the dining room table. With his five-package-per-day habit and a fifth of a Chivas Regal Scotch, he began his rampage.

He got drunk and began to run his mouth about what he called my Mammy.

I listened as long as I could until I was overcome with his inappropriate ranting. I slammed my fist into the refrigerator and told him that he had to go. I asked Phil to drive him to his truck stop.

Wilma had not seen me show a violent side of myself and was in a state of shock. A couple of days later Wilma said some unsavory things to me and I slapped her, and our relationship was over. Her sisters came over the next day and helped her move out, and I never saw Wilma again.

I moved from a two-bedroom into a one-bedroom apartment, and in a county as large as Los Angeles County, I could go out on any night of the week in the seventies and connect with a woman. Not because I was so great but because of the cultural aspect of the population.

The edge that I felt that I had over many men my age in Southern California is that I was a black man from Minnesota.

There just weren't that many black men in California that spoke with a Scandinavian accent. I'm not knocking East Coast people or Southern people either but coming out of the sixties, there were more opportunities for black people. In interviews, because I grew up in a family where we spoke fluent English, the early seventies interviewers would judge a black male's intellect on the basis of how much command of the English language he had.

As I began my training at Crocker Bank, I didn't realize two things: First, while I had ended a relationship with a slap to the face, I didn't spend five seconds worth of contemplation on my abusiveness. I just moved on without any thoughts in regard to two failed relationships. Second, this was a second shot at the management training program in banking. I should have been more serious about my career than I was, but at twenty-four years of age, I was enjoying life as a bachelor in Southern California, and living in the San Fernando Valley was wonderful.

My bachelorhood gave me a good reason not to take my own personal inventory because even though I was studying the occult and esoteric, I was also a girl watcher of the first degree.

While I wasn't mature, I worked every day on a respectable job, and I was clean-cut and honest.

In 1974, the gas crunch was hurting the automobile business, so I made the switch at the right time.

I worked at a branch in Mission Hills and the next place at the Wilshire Stoner branch in Brentwood, California. I was training in as a loan interviewer and was in the right place at the right time when the existing assistant loan manager fell out of favor, and the loan manager Rocco Romano asked if he could hire me as his assistant.

They offered me the job, and I took it and worked hard. In the midseventies, Brentwood was what it is now—upscale. The branch where I worked celebrities like Jimmy Lennon, Cannonball Adderley, Mark Harmon, to name of few, would come in to do their banking. I was placed on a special assignment and sent to Inglewood, California, to help as part of a team of loan collectors to dramatically lower their delinquency rates. I was in Inglewood for three months and returned to the Brentwood branch, and I loved it. Rocco Romano and I got along well, and from my experiences in the automobile business with Jewish and Italian people, they both value honesty and trust. I always give both, so I did well.

I worked hard for Rocco, and yet one day the branch manager and Rocco came to me and told me that against their wishes I was being transferred back to the valley to a Van Nuys branch. What they disclosed to me was that a major depositor had a problem with a black man sitting in my chair.

I told them I understood and thanked them for their honesty, and in 1974, I was not O. J. Simpson. Someone didn't want to see me in that neighborhood. I saw by the look on the branch manager's face that he knew that what was going on was unfair. Rocco was upset, but let's face it, money talks. I accepted their action and the transfer to the Van Nuys branch.

Since I lived only a mile away in Panorama City, I didn't mind. The automobile business was being greatly affected by the rising price of gasoline and oil. I had made the switch at the right time, and a paycheck that I could count on through a salary was wonderful during this gas crunch period.

I didn't dwell on my removal from my job in Brentwood because I understood racism in Southern California. I had already been one of the pioneers in auto sales in Burbank, North Hollywood, Highland Park and in banking, Mission Hills, California, Brentwood, and now Van Nuys. Growing up in the 98 percent Northern European Minnesota prepared me for the culture of Southern California.

In business in California, you have to be exceptional and striving to become the best at all times, or you are history, period.

The most important aspect is money, and the banking business is hand in hand with the automobile business.

On a cultural level from working in both fields, I learned most of what I learned from Jews and Italians because I was young, educated, and most importantly 100 percent trustworthy. I made a lot of money with them, and the fact that they were New York transplants meant that they were sharp when it came to sizing up people.

I learned what I learned in the automobile business from some of the sharpest salespeople I ever knew.

I always had the edge over most salesmen because I understood the store's typical ways most of the society that I worked in saw me and that I was always way ahead of them because I had learned from the best.

South California suburban branch banking in the seventies was no different from the banking I had performed in Minnesota.

During this period, my Scandinavian diction was perceived as higher intellect for a black man.

It was in the fall of 1974 that I would meet Cheryl Marshall from Philadelphia, Pennsylvania.

I say this because Cheryl was one of the most beautiful women I ever met before or since I met her. I met her on a Saturday afternoon.

I always drove into the black area of Los Angeles for a haircut, and in this case my barber was a man named Bill Joiner of Head Hunters Salon on Santa Barbara Avenue and Crenshaw Boulevard. Joiner had the most enjoyable experience I've ever had at the barbershop.

Afterward, I knew him well enough to go in the back room and get a scotch on the rocks and wait my turn to get my hair attended to. Because I lived in a neighborhood in the San Fernando Valley that was predominately Northern European and Jewish, I loved going to the barbershop in the black community because I enjoyed the atmosphere and spirituality of my people. As I was leaving the shop and driving down Crenshaw Boulevard, I got gas at a Union 76 Station before the Santa Monica freeway.

As I was walking back to my car, I saw Cheryl Marshall coming down Crenshaw crying. I have always been spontaneous, so I asked her to join me in my brand-new 1974 Mustang Ghia (silver on silver in silver).

I told her that there was no reason for her to be crying. She had a sister (Toni) working inside at the station, and she had to go inside.

I went in with her, and her sister told her that she'd talked to me on several occasions and that I was "cool."

Cheryl had gone to Oregon State University and just got dumped by her boyfriend for another woman. I looked at Cheryl and thought to myself, *This woman is an eleven on a scale of one through ten. Someone is crazy.*

She asked me if I knew who Bobby Moore was. I told her I did, and she told me that he had changed his name to Ahmad Rashad. We drove around for several hours and got a bite to eat, and I dropped her off at her apartment in North Hollywood. We got together many times, and yet because of her heartbreak I just liked being with her.

On one occasion she bought my ticket to join her at The Forum for a Lakers game in what I could see were great seats. She ordered two glasses of wine, and I had never sat at a basketball game and enjoyed a glass of wine with such a pretty woman.

After the game, she took me to a supper club on Warner Boulevard next to NBC studios. This woman was first class in every way.

I enjoyed just a nice time-sharing dinner or just sitting and talking with each other. I'd pick her up at her place and bring her to my apartment for dinner and a football game, and Cheryl not only knew the game but knew all the referee's signals also and would see a play and jump off the couch and perform the right signal before the referee did. One evening when I was dropping Cheryl at her place in North Hollywood, we were just sitting and talking in the parking lot in my car when pump rifles came in each window pointed at our temples.

A policeman ordered me to provide my auto registration and driver's license. I showed both plus my Crocker Bank business card identifying me as a loan manager of the Van Nuys branch.

The policeman took my information and radioed in, and as he was walking back to my car, I heard him discussing Cheryl's race and the fact that she wasn't a white woman. When he handed me my identification back, I asked him what this was all about. With five squad cars for backup, there must be a good explanation for this. The officer explained to me that there had been a robbery in the neighborhood, and the car matched the description of my car. Cheryl got out and went into her building, and I drove home thinking, *Only in LA.*

It was right about this time when I was invited to what I'd like to refer to as a scull session, where a group of guys get together and just talk or exchange information.

I attended, we discussed many subjects, and I brought the esoteric subject to the table. Cheryl Marshall had exposed me to the books of *Tuesday Lobsang Rampa*. She explained to me that life is a purification process of the self. She helped me take my first astral projection trip. She played an album by a group called Weather Report, and the album was called *Mysterious Traveler*. She also gave me insight into jazz music on a deeper level than I'd known.

With Cheryl's teachings, I was quite knowledgeable in my skull sessions, and before long I was aware of the fact that these men were recruiting me into the Nation of Islam.

I was familiar with the teachings of Malcolm X and the Nation. My only objection to their teachings was their stance on Northern European people. Their view of all whites was the devil. I had a different background from my Minnesota upbringing and wasn't going to be a part of this kind of thinking, and I told them so and left. In a few months, Elijah Muhammed passed away, and his son started something called Islam in the West. In sixteen consecutive Sundays, mosque 27, through closed circuit television, instructed its members on Muslims being of European heritage in Mecca praying with he and Malcom.

It wasn't long before I was evolving into an Islamic understanding.

It was in early spring when I looked in the Muslim book of names and chose the name Kashif Akbar Ali. Kashif means discoverer or revealer; Akbar highest or attribute of God; Ali, elevated one.

I continued to study with a man named John Isaac Thompson of Boston, who met Malcolm and converted to become Rashad Rashada.

I learned an enormous amount of knowledge and would grow in more ways than one.

I was a believer in God before I became a Muslim, which in English means *believer*, but many have been programmed to be afraid of Arabic words. Islam in English translates to "one who totally commits to the will of God."

Having been a Christian all my life, I was always aware of God's presence in my life. Islam gave me a ritual of discipline that I had never had before. I was becoming more aware inside my being. At the same time, I began going to psychic readers.

Willie and Hazel Johnson took me to see Lorraine the tea-leaf lady. I cannot remember the exact words that she said to me in the first reading, but I had always had very gifted readers that were able to show me my future in advance. Living in Los Angeles as a bachelor gave me many opportunities to meet women and that I did; having the availability of a psychic who can see my future with my date come in handy many times.

When I look back on who I was at twenty-seven years of age, I'd say advanced in some ways and yet very immature in many aspects that were obvious to the women that I came in contact with. By this I mean that I lacked the ability to create, nurture, and develop a relationship.

I couldn't go the distance, but my relationships were sprints. I was looking for my soul mate, but I wasn't looking for a wife.

Working for Crocker Bank and being single gave me a lot of opportunities to enjoy my weekends.

As 1974 turned to 1975, I went to work and to the basketball court at a park not far from my apartment in Panorama City.

I go home, change from my suit to my basketball gear, and play full court three on three until 10:00 p.m. and go back home and relax in the swimming pool. My biggest hobby was music of all kinds, depending on my mood.

I spent many evenings with female company at my apartment with a bottle of wine and good music coming from the stereo, but beyond sleeping together, I lacked the ability to close the deal.

To be honest, Los Angeles has so many beautiful women that it's overwhelming to say the least.

CHAPTER
Twenty-Four

In the fall of 1975, I decided to fly back to Minneapolis and stay at my mother and her husband's home in Mendota Heights, Minnesota. Going back home was always emotional for me because it was like revisiting the past.

I explained my Islamic name and religion to my mother, and she still didn't have a clue. When she introduced me as her son, she would say, "What was your name again?"

It was embarrassing for me because she could have tried to understand. She wasn't referring to Ali as Cassius Clay.

While I was in town, I thought I'd look in on Mr. and Mrs. Charles Martin. They were, in a big sense, surrogate parents to me because they knew my family and background. Mr. Martin shared a Freemasonry background with my father, and they as a couple knew everyone in every aspect of my families. They gave me love, and from the age of sixteen years, I always checked in on them for guidance. In high school, I dated two of their daughters and in the end became just friends to all of them.

On this visit in the fall of 1975 would be a turning point in my life.

This is similar to that day at the beach in 1966 when I felt sorry for a girl and began a "rescue" relationship that would affect the rest of my life. As I sat talking with the Martins that evening in Minneapolis, I inquired about their four offspring. They told me about their daughter Marilyn. Mr. Martin tightened up as Mrs. Martin told me to go visit Marilyn while I was in town. I left their house after calling Marilyn and getting the address, and I drove over to meet her. She answered the door, and I went inside her apartment and sat down.

Out of the bedroom came Shannon, age five, and Shane, age three. I have always been a sucker for kids and the fact that her boys were beautiful in looks. I hadn't seen Marilyn in about six years, and we were both divorced.

Marilyn and I talked well into the night, and I left and drove back to my mother's home. I should have gone on about my business and left to go back to California where I belonged, but no, I had to feel sorry for Marilyn and her kids living below her means. There were so many, many stop signs, but I made a big mistake by thinking I could rescue someone from their destiny.

I believe that it was the combination of going home, which is always nostalgic for me, emotionally, connecting with the Martins, and seeing Marilyn for the first time in years.

It was to me a mistake on my part because I was, to me, going back in time in my own mind without looking at the red flags. The first flag was that she was not working to provide for those two sons she had. The second was that I didn't recognize Mr. Martin's obvious resistance. Third was that I wasn't emotionally stable enough to be a male role model to two boys, and I was an extremist, wherein I only knew that I could always leave.

I should have told her that it was great seeing her again, but for what reason I will never know, I felt compelled to reach out and help Marilyn.

I got on the plane, and when I landed in LA, I called Marilyn and began a long-distance relationship that would have a long-lasting effect on even more people because of my bizarre abusive behavior that was hidden by my independent distant attitude disguised as being a bachelor who would move on at the least provocation. I would dissolve the relationship if I saw an argument coming.

I had absolutely no idea of how to resolve a conflict with a woman. I only knew to leave. I could always find someone new.

My job as an assistant installment loan manager was going well, and other than being a bit lonely as I always have in the fall season, I stayed in touch with Marilyn.

Somehow, I felt that I owed her some sort of aid. Anyone that I confided in thought I was crazy to want a woman with kids who wasn't doing anything to create a better life for herself.

Meanwhile I was having some deep conversations with my Muslim friends. Rashad lived a very clean life with a wife and a son in a nice house in a nice part of Pacoima.

I was twenty-seven, and he was thirty-three at the time and had been in the Nation of Islam but understood Malcolm's conversation after his hajj to Mecca—the understanding that one cannot paint all cultures with a broad brush and all white people are not devils.

In reality, I was in a sense becoming two people: William Commodore and Kashif Ali.

I worked after hours at the branch, and because I had a key, I could let myself into work. I'd work for about an hour and call Marilyn back in Minneapolis and chat. Marilyn even came to Los Angeles and stayed with me for a week. I lost my focus with reality and by Thanksgiving lost my job at the bank, and it was pure stupidity on my part, but Christmas came and went.

I had been seeing Rashad's sister Charlotte from Delaware and keeping her at a distance while I was still calling Marilyn.

Since I was unemployed, I went to an executive search firm in Century City, California, called Group Four. The owner saw something in my résumé because he offered me a position in his firm.

I began to learn yet another art—headhunting. I was working for about a month when my savings was low, and Charlotte asked me to move in with her.

It was a perfect fit because Rashad and I were close friends, and he was delighted to see me with his sister.

Charlotte was the perfect Muslim wife to me, and yet because I was so wild, I couldn't appreciate her. My mind was still on Marilyn back home. After two months at Group Four, I was waiting on a commission check when my cousin Phillip was calling to let me know the gas crunch was over and the general manager and team were at a dealership called Holmes Tuttle Ford in Hollywood.

My cousin and I had already worked with these men at two dealerships, and I was being asked because I had a reputation for selling a lot of cars.

Holmes Tuttle Ford sat on the corner of Beverly and Labrea, and across the street was A&M Records. I had heard that Quincy Jones and Herb Alpert owned the company.

Mr. Holmes Tuttle was at the time a man of enormous wealth who owned 75 percent of Trans World Airlines and financed Ronald Reagan to run for governor of California and presidency of the United States.

To me, Mr. Tuttle resembled the actor Ray Milland in looks. He was a Conservative Republican, and the only reason that my cousin and I were accepted as salesmen in Hollywood in the seventies was our established record of sales ability. I was placed on the used car lot that had six salesmen, and the sales manager was an ex-policeman named Chuck Crockett. The salesmen were older established salesmen, who were great salesmen and very intellectual.

The used cars were top-notch and in great shape and easy to sell. I was happy to be selling used cars because in the automobile business, no two cars are the same, and so that there is no comparison between two used cars. The prices on the used cars were not marked for the customer to see, but the salesman can decipher the code on the windshield. Written in the code was the asking price of the car.

The markup was in most cases a thousand dollars. This gave the salesman room to negotiate. I would in most cases add an additional one thousand dollars so that I had more after negotiations were over.

I wish that I had been more mature because I was arrogant once I began a streak of sales.

The men I was working with were seasoned veterans who had consistently been successful month after month, year after year.

I didn't realize that I was as impulse-oriented as I was because I wasn't really processing my own behavior.

I had been successful at two dealerships within the organization, and my cousin and I overcame any objections because of our race with our professionalism and sales ability.

CHAPTER
Twenty-Five

This was the summer of 1976, and it was a bicentennial year. I had met a man named Muntu Umoja, and we began hanging out together when I wasn't with Rashad. I was making good money selling cars and meeting pretty women at a pace that was record setting for me, and I had a swagger to my attitude.

I was living with Charlotte, who by now had changed her name to Hanna, and while I was working long hours, she had some impressive meals for me when I got in. I still called Marilyn back in Minneapolis from time to time to see how she was doing. She had gotten a job as a customer service representative with the bus company. She went to work at 4:00 p.m. and finished at 1:00 a.m. The kids were watched by her parents.

I should've left well enough alone, but I was impulsive.

The year 1976 was probably my best summer in California because I was so very active, and I had experiences that in later years were very memorable.

One of the memories was of an actor named Scoey Mitchell, who was one of the pioneers of black actors in Hollywood, who came in the dealership to sell his white BMW.

What I remember was that he was a very dignified man with a presence. He had a very pretty dignified wife, and they seemed very happy.

What I remember most about Mr. Mitchell is that he was the first person to teach me not to use the word *nigger*.

I was driving somewhere in Hollywood and saw him getting out of his car, and I yelled out, "What's happening, nigger?"

He gave me a look that put my young ass in my place and gave me a lecture on that word and how I'd better respect him. He wasn't angry, just dignified. Thank you, Mr. Mitchell.

One of the highlights of being in that dealership was that many famous people bought their cars there. Across the street was A&M Records, where Quincy Jones and Herb Alpert were. Roscoe DeValt was in security there, and after I got to know him, he allowed me to purchase albums there at a discounted price.

I never got to see Mr. Jones, and I was introduced to Mr. Jones by Pittsburgh Joe Jones, who introduced me to an album entitled *Walking in Space.*

Mr. Jones was writing scores for Hollywood's best movies among many other categories of music.

He is a masterpiece.

My cousin sold a lot of cars to many R&B artists including the Brothers Johnson and Denise Williams, whom I spoke to while she was waiting for my cousin Phil to return. She showed me her credit application, and I saw where she had been on tour with Stevie Wonder and Earth, Wind and Fire. She owned a music publishing company.

I was impressed that this woman left Gary Indiana and had accomplished so much. My cousin came back and sold her a 1976 Granada, and I told him what I thought of her, and his reply was that he had a date set up with her. I never asked him the results of their date, but a few weeks later, I was driving east on Sunset Boulevard when I passed Tower Records and I saw Denise William's album and picture on the album entitled *This Is Nicey.*

I was having a wonderful summer and would have been even more successful at work if I had paid attention to the rules of the dealership. By this I mean there was only one rule: leave the assistant office manager alone. I found this out one day when I asked my cousin who the pretty girl was in the business office.

He told me she was off limits and to don't ask any more questions.

Instead of being wise and taking heed, I was intrigued.

This impulsiveness in part began a streak of auto sales just to be able to go to the office window and come in contact with her. After about two weeks of sales, I decided to experiment. I had a book on the occult and decided to burn a candle (white) and place a piece of paper with her name on it in the flame. I went to work the next day, and Pam, the switchboard operator, called me at my desk and laughingly told me that Judy wanted to meet me.

To be honest I was dumbfounded, not to mention shocked. Judy Rivera was a very pretty twenty-five-year-old Mexican woman from San Antonio, Texas, and we began dating. Remember I was still living with Charlotte (who became Hanna). I was enjoying my bachelorhood at twenty-eight years of age and on a high that I cannot describe. Can you imagine having business cards that read salesman Skip Commodore at a time when the Commodore Computer was in vogue and when driving down Sunset Boulevard and passing Tower Records you can see on the big billboard in big letters an album with the Commodores' *Hot on the Tracks*.

I was experiencing my own self-induced joy by association. As far as I was concerned my name was popular.

CHAPTER
Twenty-Six

In June of 1976, my friend Rashad YaYa Rashada, Muntu Umoja, and I attended an event called a jubilee.

This event was at Los Angeles Convention Center and put on by mosque 27 in Los Angeles. The chief imam was Elijah Mohammed's son Wallace, and this event was closed-circuit sent to other Mosques around the nation.

I've been to a few events in my lifetime, but this ranks at the top of my list. This Sunday the center was packed, and to list all the important people who attended in person would take too long.

Imam W. D. Muhammad spoke and explained that this event was a bringing together in fellowship members of the People's Temple of the city of San Francisco and members of Mosque 27—Christians and Muslims. The ushers were Muslim and Christians standing side by side. It was a sight to see, and yet it was never reported in any local publication or on the news stations. I looked a couple of rows from where I was sitting and saw Muhammad Ali's ex-wife Khaliah sitting not far from me and thought to myself, "She is absolutely beautiful." In my opinion, Muhammed should have stayed with her, but who am I to judge anyone?

The keynote speaker at the event following W. D. Muhammed was a man named Jim Jones.

Yes, that Jim Jones.

Reverend Jim Jones began an oratory that mesmerized me, and I was moved.

I thoroughly believe that many in the audience that day were moved by his speaking ability.

My friend Muntu was moved enough to suggest that we go to Guyana and live. Three months later I found out that Reverend Jim

Jones murdered almost a thousand followers on cyanide-laced Kool-Aid. I was shocked that a man with so much charisma could do what he did.

About a week after the jubilee, a girl that I had sold a car to named Gilda Brooks invited me to go with her and her girlfriend to Pirates Cove. I took Muntu with me. Pirate Cove was a popular nude beach at the time, and at twenty-eight years old I was curious. When we got there, Muntu and I were not going to take our cut-off shorts off, so the girls just bared their breasts. Everyone else on the beach was fully naked, and to be honest it was an overrated experience. That night I took Judy to Redondo Beach, and after a meal we sat in the car on the ocean. We talked until we both fell asleep and were awakened by the next morning's sunlight.

Judy realized that she would be late for work if she went home to prepare for work, so she went straight to work. My shift started at 3:00 p.m. so I just drove back to my apartment. At about 1:30 p.m., my cousin called me to tell me that a trap had been set for me at work. It seems that someone saw a disheveled Judy come to work and would be blaming her being with me the night before being the reason.

My cousin still hadn't told me what all this secrecy was about.

Nevertheless, I phoned Gilda Brooks whom I'd been with that afternoon at Pirates Cove. I asked Gilda to say that after an afternoon at Pirate's Cove, she and I spent the night together at her place. I got to the used car lot at 2:45 p.m., and I could tell by the faces of the other salesmen that I was walking into a trap and everyone was salivating, waiting for my demise. I walked into my office and prepared for my shift, and the used car manager Mr. Chuck Crocket demanded that I come to his office immediately.

I walked in, and Chuck had the expression on his face that I confirmed the overconfident arrogance of an ex-LAPD police officer displays when they have their case solved. Mr. Crocket (twenty years on the force before his retirement) asked me if I didn't mind telling him what I did yesterday on my day off.

I prefaced my response with the fact that my activities on my off day were my personal business, but I was with a woman that I'd sold a car to Gilda Brooks and that we had gone to Pirate's Cove (the nude beach) together and I had spent the night at her place.

Mr. Crockett had her sold deal papers in front of him with other recent deals, and he pulled the numbers for Gilda's job and residence. He called her at work and, after reintroducing himself to her, asked her what she had done the day before. Gilda told him what I wanted her to, and I could tell by the way Mr. Crockett's face and neck turned red that the trap had been sprung.

I then asked him why I had to divulge my private business like that. He explained that there had been a suspicion that I had been out with someone that was off-limits. I then asked him who this was that I was supposed to have been with. His response was "I didn't want to know." I'd dodged a bullet, but as mindless as I was at the time, I found the experience kind of exciting. I later found out that Judy was the property of the vice president Mr. Ray P., who had a wife and kids. You'd think that I'd have had the sense to leave Judy alone, but not Kashif, the maverick Muslim Convert.

I was blinded by my own ego and couldn't see the red flags blowing in the wind in front of me.

It seems the vice president decided to hire a private detective to watch Judy and I. I asked Judy about her relationship with him and she didn't answer me, and I was so dumb I couldn't see the big red flag in front of me.

Judy enjoyed the excitement, and we kept seeing each other. When her mother and grandfather moved to Los Angeles from San Antonio, Texas, Judy introduced me to them.

I moved from Charlotte's (Hanna's) place into an apartment in Hollywood (525 South Ardmore on Wilshire Boulevard).

At work I was selling a lot of cars and was totally unaware of the plotting that was taking place to get rid of me. I was transferred from the used car lot to the new car lot across the street.

My new car manager was an Italian named Pete Lentini, and he worked at Universal Ford in North Hollywood and knew my track record within the organization that we worked for.

As I've already said, I have had my best business relations with Italians and Jewish people because I had a reputation for being trustworthy. My dealings with them were always very positive. Mr. Robinson (Sugar Ray) had a great relationship with Mr. Sinatra, and I trust that.

Pete was honest with me when he said that my time with the dealership was short because the vice president's plan was to get rid of me as soon as my selling streak ended.

Pete told me that we'd have fun while it lasted.

The general manager Mr. Frank Ring point-blank told me that my ruse with Gilda was only a temporary fix, but I couldn't continue, in his words, to "mess with the boss's puss" and not have a problem. My days were numbered at Holmes Tuttle Ford, but not without my discussing my meeting to the legendary Mr. Ollie Matson.

CHAPTER
Twenty-Seven

I came to work this particular afternoon, and there was a man sitting in the chair next to my desk. I asked him if I could help him.

He introduced himself as Ollie Matson and that he'd been a pretty good football player and Olympian. He told me his story and how many players (nine) the Las Angeles Rams traded for him, and as I sat, I listened to this hall-of-fame player. I almost relived my life as he talked to me. My sales manager came up to me and wanted to know what the purpose of my customer was and that I'd been listening for two hours without a credit application being filled out, to see if I was wasting my time.

I filled out the application as I asked Mr. Matson for the information. I needed to qualify him for a purchase. I took the application to my sales manager, and after we ran his credit, I was told if he didn't have a cosigner and a lot of money for a down payment, there was nothing I could do for him. I went back and informed Mr. Matson of our requirements for him, and he had no money for a down payment or cosigner. Mr. Matson was probably the kindest man I had met next to Mr. Sugar Ray Robinson.

When I broke the news to Mr. Matson, he talked to me for another hour and fifteen minutes before my sales Manager came and told Mr. Matson what the cold hard facts were. Mr. Matson was very gracious and classy and thanked us for our time and left. I went to the men's room and cried my twenty-eight-year-old eyes out.

I'll never forget the experience. Meanwhile, the general manager called me into his office and told me the vice president of the dealership wanted to get rid of me and that no matter how many cars I sold, the general manager was supposed to make sure I finished in the bottom three and supposedly all three of us had to leave.

I had been seeing Judy every evening, and if I was being watched, I was so stupid I wasn't hiding anything. Pete was right about the sales being rigged because my sales mysteriously began to become manipulated. By this I mean I'd sell a car and agree on a date and time for delivery and get to the dealership and discover that my customer had been told to come in and take delivery of the car from another salesman, which meant I'd have to share the sale and the commission with another salesman even though I did all the work.

Pete set me up for an interview at Miller Datsun in the valley, and I moved on but kept seeing Judy. I started on Monday at the Datsun store, but my head wasn't really in it. I was a Ford man, and I couldn't get excited about Datsun.

They gave me a B210 model for a demonstrator, but I wasn't impressed.

After about a month, I wasn't selling at the pace I could have and went back to my apartment in Hollywood and called my mother in Minneapolis and asked if I could stay with her and her husband for a few months.

I packed my things and asked my friend Rashad to store my belongings in his garage until I came back. A few people came to my apartment to keep me from leaving, but I had my mind made up.

I needed a break.

CHAPTER
Twenty-Eight

As I boarded the red-eye flight and sat down, I remember thinking to myself maybe LA was too much for the man. As soon as
I landed in Minneapolis, my first thought was that things seemed to
move so much slower, and the city of Minneapolis was much smaller
in size.

I called Marilyn and borrowed my mother's car and went to
her mother's house, where she and her two sons were living. It was
nice to see her parents because they were very kind to me. I got in
town on a Saturday morning, and on Monday I went to the city
of Bloomington and the city of Richfield to get operator's licenses
because I was about to drive the 5:00 p.m. to 5:00 a.m. shift for my
mother's husband as we shared driving a taxicab. Southwest Taxi was
now called Suburban Taxi. I drove for my mother's husband, so I had
no dealings with the people in the office. Once again, I was working
in the suburbs, and in the midseventies the Bloomington strip was
full of action. In those days, Bloomington and Richfield were full
of saunas that males could frequent for massages and other forms of
entertainment.

Whenever I got a male from the various hotels and motels on
the strip that inquired, I would steer him to the sauna that paid me
ten dollars and would call the cab company and tell them to send me
for the return trip. I enjoyed working nights on the strip because each
shift was full of surprises.

Marilyn was working the 4:00 p.m. to 1:00 a.m. shift at the
MTC bus company answering phones and dispatching customers.
My pace had slowed down considerably in coming back home. At
1:00 a.m., I would pick Marilyn up and we'd have a bite to eat at
whatever was open. We would go back to her parents' house, and I'd

leave around 4:30 a.m. and arrive to my mother's place in Mendota Heights to give the cab to her husband for his daily shift.

On one occasion, someone who knew that I was visiting Marilyn in that cab slashed the tires. My mother's husband seemed to know who did it and connected it to my ex-wife. After all, Marilyn had been one of my ex's childhood girlfriends.

I had a conversation with my mother about my conversion from Christianity to Islam, and she decided that I had no one to relate to who was a Muslim.

One afternoon she decided to call her friends the Gilliams (Frank Gilliam, director of player personnel for the Minnesota Vikings) to see if Ahmad Rashad could call me because he also was a Muslim.

I was taking a nap one afternoon when the phone rang, and my mother handed it to me. On the other end of the line was Ahmad Rashad introducing himself, and his question in the same breath was if I was a Sunni Muslim. When I told him that I was a follower of W. D. Muhammad and follower of Islam in the West, I could hear his tone turn to disinterest because he was following a different sect. In fairness, we were both young, and I didn't get to ask him about Cheryl Marshall at Oregon. I did sit in subzero temperatures at Metropolitan Stadium to watch them beat a Ram team in the playoffs.

CHAPTER
Twenty-Nine

Time would pass very quickly in Minnesota, and by February I was prepared to leave and go back to LA. I had several conversations with Judy, so I knew that she was waiting. I had entrusted my friend Rashad with my belongings, so it was just a matter of setting up shop again. To show you how brain-dead and thoughtless I was, I took my friend Chuck Martin to LA with me. He was Marilyn's younger brother. We're drinking champagne on the flight to LA, and when we landed in LA at LAX International Airport, Judy was waiting for us.

Judy was stunning and Chuck was impressed. She drove us to her apartment in Hollywood, and the three of us were at Manhattan Beach in a half an hour and eating apple cinnamon pancakes at Uncle John's Pancake House.

By 8:00 p.m., Judy told me that we had been invited to attend a private party in Laurel Canyon. It was two o'clock in the morning, and we were at a party that can only happen in LA among the wealthy.

The only way to describe it is to say that they were all there. Chuck was overwhelmed. He could only sit on the floor and take it all in.

Judy had taken us to the type of Hollywood Hills party where you had to know someone to be in this scene and a mixture of people in one place. I'd learned many years ago that whenever you encounter a situation that you have no cognitive point of reference, you have to act as if it's no big deal and show no emotion, even if your mind is totally blown. Judy was taking me to this scene to see my response. I played my role and acted as though I didn't recognize the personalities that I was privileged to be with for the evening. My friend

Chuck was viewing life in the fast lane and told me later that he was astonished.

The next day Judy, Chuck, and I went to my favorite basketball court in Panorama City, and we played for a few hours and went back to Judy's place. I hadn't told Chuck any of my plans before we flew to Los Angeles, and I'd just left his sister in Minneapolis and the personality he saw in Minneapolis and my transition to bachelorhood. I was trying to show him how cool I was when in reality I was showing my fraudulent character and untrustworthy nature.

I left Judy's place and rented a motel room in Sepulveda and a truck for transportation.

I left Chuck at the motel room and spent the night at Judy's. When I returned the next day, Chuck was still sleeping at 2:00 p.m., and that was when he informed me that last night after I left, he heard partying down the hall and went down to see what was going on. He went down and was invited to join the party. He said all the drugs were there and that he enjoyed the people and left at about 9:00 a.m. He told me that when he asked them who they were, he was told by some guy named Jerry that they were the Grateful Dead.

Chuck caught a plane back to Minneapolis, and I got a sales job at Culver Motors Ford and began working on a used car lot. I had a lot on my mind and was calling Marilyn back in Minneapolis and seeing Judy at the same time. I drove to Lancaster to see my favorite tea-leaf reader named Lorraine. Whenever I needed to look into the future, I went to her for direction. Lorraine was extremely accurate, and on my own I went to her to see into the woman that I had met. This particular visit I wanted to see my future with Marilyn.

Lorraine had the most painful look on her face when she warned me not to bring Marilyn out before August. This was the end of April, and in my confused state of mind, I was acting upon things without thinking.

I wasn't grounded in any way and was seeing two women at the same time and not being honest with either one of them.

To compound my problem, I had become Kashif Ali after work and Skip Commodore by day selling cars. I was not living an honest life, but I wasn't even being honest enough with myself to see my own dishonesty.

I was existing and not living honestly. I was calling Marilyn on Judy's phone and placing calls from work.

In reality I was emotionally unstable and ignoring all the red flags.

The real truth was that I should have dropped the idea of being with Marilyn, and if I had, she would have kept working at the bus company and eventually saved enough money to move into her own apartment from her parents' home. Somehow, I felt that I had in some way a responsibility to Marilyn even though I wasn't being completely honest with her.

I didn't trust Judy because she never came clean about being the vice president's mistress.

In truth we were learning to understand each other's culture, and we had a sexual relationship. I had enough of a relationship with her to meet her mother and grandfather and maybe something could have developed in time, but for some unknown reason, I was in a hurry.

I probably should have let both women go, and yet I complicated their lives for no reason.

At one point I asked Judy to marry me, and her response was that it was too soon. I had my answer, and even though the tea-leaf reader Lorraine had warned me about bringing Marilyn out before August, I cast all caution to the wind and made plans to bring Marilyn out. People who knew me weren't telling me that I wasn't acting rationally; they just watched.

I had no real focus but was living a complete contradiction.

I had no problem selling cars and making money, but for some reason I was lonely and wanted to be in a relationship even though I had no tools to build with.

CHAPTER

Thirty

Marilyn and her two boys, Shannon and Shane, arrived in May, and I had rented a two-bedroom apartment in Sepulveda and bought a king-sized bed. The first night I sat up with her all night talking then showered and went to work at sunup and worked all day. I repeated the same pattern for a number of days, running on adrenaline with no real sleep or proper food. I was coming apart mentally and ignoring all the vital signs. I began to read the Quran and other books, assimilating a lot of information and running my mouth nonstop. With school starting in a few weeks I got the idea that we should be legal and planned a drive to Las Vegas to get married. We dropped the kids off at her aunt's house in Inglewood and drove to Las Vegas. We went to the courthouse and got married at the Silver Bell Wedding Chapel.

We left the chapel and went next door to the Royal Casino. We gambled at the roulette wheel and won $1,400 and got back in the car and headed for Los Angeles. By the time Monday arrived I hadn't slept and was running on adrenaline.

I went to work and was so incoherent that I was sent home to rest.

When I got home, I was lying on my back on the bed when Marilyn, my new bride, was picking ingrown hairs from my face. I was beginning to hallucinate and saw my mother's face superimposed over hers, and I freaked out.

I acted possessed as I left the apartment under the promise of buying a pack of cigarettes. The problem was that I had a pair of beige cut-off jeans and a powder-blue-and-pink striped tank top and no shoes or socks walking about a block and one half to the 7-Eleven convenience store. Instead of heading to the store, I headed for

Sepulveda Boulevard, and I was walking down the boulevard when I heard a voice tell me to take a money clip holding $130 out of my pocket and drop it in the weeds. I headed back to the 7-Eleven I was supposed to be going to, and I walked into a Chevron gas station and got in a Cadillac and drove it out of the gas station onto the street. After a block, I regained my senses and got out of the car, and whoever the owner was tried to grab me and he was back fisted (martial arts strike) to the ground. I was walking onto the San Diego freeway when the police caught up to me and dragged me through the gravel to the squad car and put me in the back seat.

I was facedown when someone opened the door and hit the back of my head with what I believe was a blunt instrument, and I blacked out.

When I woke up, I was in a padded cell from floor to ceiling. I was naked, and I got up from the floor and went to a plexiglass window with air holes in it. I looked outside. On the floor was my torn tank top and cut-off jeans lying on the floor. I knew that I had no memory of taking my clothes off. I noticed that I had a shooting pain in my ass. I put my hand back there and felt a wet substance leaking out of my rectum, and when I put a sample on my finger and put it up to my nose, I recognized the smell of semen.

That was when I began to get angry and then went berserk in an unbelievable rage.

I yelled out the window, "You raped me, and you have no idea who you have in here!"

I noticed a metal drain in the middle of the floor, and I sat in front of it and began to bang my fists on it to make them bleed.

I licked the blood from my knuckles and licked the sweat from my body and began to bang my fists and sidekick the padded walls as I screamed at the cops outside my cell. I challenged the rapists to come get some more. They began yelling for me to quiet down.

I had already gone mad and realized that I was thirsty and needed water.

In a quiet almost childish voice, I asked for water, and I heard one of the cops yell that they were going to give me water.

When the cell door opened and the cop put a Styrofoam cup of water on the floor, I blasted him in the head with a backfist, and he slammed the door. I drank half of the water and went back to hitting and sidekicking the padded walls as I admonished the listening cops for raping me.

I would crouch over in a corner and sit Indian style and look up at the two overhead lights so my pupils would dilate to make them believe I was possessed and yell at them for more water, and each time I felt the door open I'd jump across the cell and blast the cop bringing the water. I screamed obscenities at them and challenged them for the three days they had me in that Van Nuys jail.

Meanwhile back home, Marilyn called all over trying to figure out where I went. She had my friend Danny, who was a bail bondsman at the time, looking up all my old girlfriends to see where I was.

Everyone was looking for me, and I was in the Van Nuys jail listed as John Doe X. As God would have it, Marilyn called the cops, and when she showed my picture to them, they were the cops who had arrested me. They had gone back to the San Diego freeway entrance where they had apprehended me to see if I'd left any identification in the bushes because initially I made a move with my hands that looked like I was throwing something in the bushes. That move saved me in the long run.

Marilyn said they told her where I was. When she and Danny showed up to bail me out, the police told them it was right on time because they were about to transfer me to the state hospital.

I counted twenty-seven times I hit someone coming in my cell, and I was as insane as a man could be. I had somehow climbed to the top of my padded cell and was yelling at the cops, trying to bait one of them to come in so that I could jump on him.

Danny bailed me out, and I was so wild that he and Marilyn were trying to quiet me so that they could get me out of the police station safely. I told them of the rape and wanted a doctor, but I was ignored by them. I was taken back to our apartment to rest.

They should've taken me to the doctor, who could have had a specimen of the rapist's sperm, but they were only interested in getting me to a shower and bed.

I didn't blame them because believe me, I was there, and a part of me knew I was bizarre and absolutely insane and on edge, angry to the point of total paranoia. I was almost back to earth by my newly married bride, who was witnessing insanity mixed with some logic, and when I woke up the next morning, I was rested enough for the two of us to drive to Inglewood to get the kids, who had been staying at her aunt's house so that Marilyn could find me. We took the kids back, and I was good for a night. By the second day I went to the living room and began reading the Quran and then having a conversation with Marilyn, and mind you, I cannot remember what the subject was.

I realize that one must imagine a mother of two young boys leaving a job and a comfortable place to live at her parents' home, uprooting and going to live with a man she grew up with and living with him a couple of months and running to Las Vegas and getting married and now you find out that he, your husband, is drop-dead insane. Whether she loved me and wanted to believe me or tried until she couldn't stay anymore, she stayed, and on that morning a couple of days after, I was removed from my job and coming down from the tour of the Van Nuys padded cell.

Marilyn was afraid of my behavior and took the two boys across the building to our friends Jerry and his wife. I went looking for them, and when his wife answered the door, I inquired as to if my family was there. She was then trying to shut the door as her husband, I would later find out, came into the living room with a .357 Magnum. I let his wife shut the door on me, and I went back to our apartment. Upon noticing that I had locked myself out, I grabbed the rail on this second-floor complex, put the most impressive back-kick on the locked door, and destroyed the door and most of its supporting frame. I went into the living room, sat down, put a pair of headphones on, and put a jazz album on. The police came and tapped me on the shoulder, and after I took my headphones off one of them asked me what happened to the door. My reply was that I had locked myself out. I guess they went back to my wife and told her that I seemed stable and under control but that she could call the Van Nuys facility for people who matched my description. In short, people who had gone nuts. She knew I hadn't done any drugs or alcohol, and my drug of choice was marijuana.

I had even turned her down when she told me of one of her girlfriend's giving her something called yellow barrel acid and wanted to know if I wanted to try it with her on our honeymoon.

My wife called my cousin Phil, who came and was given the job of committing me to this facility in Van Nuys for seventy-two hours. My cousin showed up, and after surveying the damage to the property and then seeing me on the headphones listening to "Sun Goddess" by Ramsey Lewis, he became confused, but he was on a mission.

He asked me to go with him for a ride. When I got in the car, as we rode, he began to explain his alcoholism to me and the pressure he was under. As I listened to him, I could see and feel his fear of me and especially after he saw what I had done to the door and doorframe back at the apartment. We got to the care facility, and he signed me in and got the hell out of there as fast as he could. After he left, the people led me into a room where I lay down and they gave me sleeping sedatives. I was on seventy-two-hour hold, and a doctor came in, after I had slept for what could be deemed rested, to tell me that my rest would be monitored and that I'd be out in seventy-two hours if I passed evaluation.

They had me on Thorazine, and twenty-four hours before I was dismissed, they took me off. When I was discharged, I found out that Marilyn and the kids had relocated to her aunt's place in Inglewood. It seems that when the landlord saw my damage to their apartment door and frame, we were asked to leave and that the four-hundred-dollar deposit that I gave them would more than cover the damage. Everyone referred to my "episode" as a nervous breakdown. In my mind I knew that I had stayed awake for too long a period to not go insane. I realized that my behavior had been bizarre and that my trip through the Van Nuys jail system compounded my already bizarre thought process. All of it seemed like one long LSD trip. Marilyn, Shannon, Shane, and I now lived with Marilyn's aunt, uncle, and two sons. They were caretakers of an apartment complex and were kind enough to take us in. I was under the influence of whatever my discharging prescription called for and had no real coherence.

I was coherent enough to see that my cousin, my friend Danny, Marilyn, and her aunt and uncle were discussing my sanity on a regular basis. I slept in a bedroom that Marilyn and I shared but had very little contact for a few days. Marilyn's parents back in Minneapolis were calling and checking also. I was under a microscope to say the least but also under the power of what everyone around me collectively decided is normal or abnormal.

A part of me also realized that all of what everyone believed was fueled by Marilyn's description of me. In fairness to my wife, she had been through quite a bit on an emotional and psychological level.

She was uprooted to be with what seemed like the strongest person she knew that went nuts after she married him.

Her father wanted to know if I had been violent to her, and when told no by his daughter, he became supportive and sent her and the kids to stay with his sister and her husband. After a few days went by, my wife's aunt began conferring with my cousin and friend Danny about the fact that my wife wasn't showing any signs of attempting to do something to produce money toward helping her husband.

My cousin, who was keeping my mother posted back in Minneapolis, was being told by my mother that my ex-wife had said that Marilyn and my marriage was a marriage made in heaven because Marilyn was lazy.

After everyone discussed Marilyn's character, they made their determination.

I was told that since I had never shown insane tendencies before taking on my new wife and kids, then it must be them.

I was advised to send Marilyn and her kids back to Minnesota and move on.

From hindsight, it was probably best for all those affected by my behavior up to that point and in the next four years to come. My focus was on saving Marilyn and the kids instead of the most obvious reality: she shouldn't have been with me and should have gotten an annulment and moved on with her life.

I take the blame for her staying because I was trying to convince her that we would win.

Everyone was in a state of confusion over what to do with Marilyn and me.

The main question was whether or not I was sane or insane.

I remember one night when I was drugged and sleeping and they tried to wake me up to watch Muhammed Ali versus Ernie Shavers on television, and I slept through the entire fight. Later that night I got up and went to the bathroom and was stretching and exercising my dormant muscles in the dark when Uncle came in, was startled, overreacted, and ran out of the bathroom.

His fear was the beginning of a domino effect that woke up everyone, and with the lights on, they all overreacted to what they thought was a violent confrontation in the making. The aunt called my friend Danny, and I became angry at everyone discussing and thinking that they can control me and my activities.

The next thing I knew the state hospital boys had me in restraints, and in front of four kids and all the adults I was carried off to Metropolitan State Hospital. I had never related to restraints in any way, but obviously if someone makes the call on you and they come and observe your behavior and see that you are irrational, then they do what they have to do.

I woke up in a bed with restraints on me in a room by myself. Eventually some people looked through the eyeholes of a small window on my door and saw that I was awake, and after talking to me, they removed the restraints and told me that they were allowing me to join the rest of the population and I should behave myself. I walked out into what was a large room with furniture and television and ping-pong tables and many chairs.

I looked around me at all the people in the room and at what I describe today as different states of consciousness.

I went to the drinking fountain and drank what to me seemed like an incredible amount of water, and when I took a breath, a man walked up to me and said, "The thirst is from the lithium they gave you to calm you down." He introduced himself to me as Steve Acorn. He told me that I should begin to go to the bathroom and drink hot water to flush the drugs out of my system. At medication time, he told me to hide the pills in my mouth and go back to the bathroom and spit the pills out in the toilet and drink some more hot water. In a few hours, my head was clear, and I began to realize that my emotions had landed me in a state hospital.

Soon it was Kool-Aid and cookie time, and I fed myself from the tray that the lady brought around. Steve Acorn kept me company nonstop, giving me useful information about what I had to do to survive and get released from this place.

At that point I began to do standing exercises and breathing.

I know now that he was a guardian that showed me a clear path back to the world outside. Soon it was the lunch hour, and soon it would be medication time. In my case, a doctor met me in my room and interviewed me and transferred me into a room with a bed. I went back to the population, and Steve Acorn came back and we conversed.

He told me that he took a knife and killed his mother's dogs in a fit of rage. He told he had a brown belt in karate and began to show me the basics and reminded me that our movements had to be very slow and deliberate or the monitors would react. We practiced for hours, and soon it was dinnertime and back to practice until medication time. Then we talked for hours. Soon my seventy-two-hour hold was coming to a close, and the doctor interviewed me and discharged me. My former sales manager Joe Miller of Culver Motors Ford came and gave me a ride back to Marilyn and the kids. He gave me a fifty-dollar bill and an ounce of very good marijuana and a lead to Westwood AMC and told me to see Pete Lentini. Joe was Jewish and Pete was Italian, and I had shown both my character and my trustworthiness to both and I had a job. I used fifty dollars to rent a fifteen-dollar-a-day kitchenette room in Inglewood.

I took the demo I got after being hired at Westwood AMC by Pete and picked up Marilyn and the kids, and we had a residence of our own.

I still don't know how we paid that fifteen dollars a night and ate, but we did.

The kids sat on the bed and watched television, and Marilyn and I played dominos.

There was only one problem, and that was that I had lost my confidence and my ability to sell cars.

Pete noticed this and felt it was because I didn't believe in the product.

Looking back, I don't think it was the product. It was me and my not having fully recovered from all that I had been through in such a short period of time. I was on the sales floor when Pete told me there was a call in my office.

When I picked up the phone, it was my grandmother in Minneapolis whom I always called Guy. She asked me if I was standing, and when I told her that I was sitting at my desk, she then told me that my father had died that morning on the operating table during an operation to remove a bad lung.

She checked to see if I was all right and told me she'd call back. I went numb and to this day never shed but one tear.

He was a five-pack-a-day smoker who developed fluid in one of his lungs that had to be removed. During the operation, the surgeon cut his heart by mistake, and he lay there and bled to death. I can only say that I really don't know how I did my grieving about my father, but I saw how everyone in my family reacted. That weekend Marilyn and the kids and I drove up to his apartment in Berkeley.

When we got there, my grandmother, my two uncles, and my father's wife were in the apartment going through his things.

I just stood and watched as one of my father's twin brothers went through my father's best clothes for his own benefit and the others went through the rest of his belongings looking for something of worth. These true buzzards were true to their nature exercising their pecking order.

My father's wife was crying and snotting as she held my father's Navy cap.

All in all, I received about five well-worn T-shirts, some outdated ties, a picture of his sixty-thousand-dollar tractor, and a hug. I forgot a plaque that read, "Blessed are those who expect nothing, for they shall not be disappointed."

I drove my family back to Los Angeles with my inheritance and spent a lot of time reliving the highs and lows of our relationship.

As I drove, I processed what I'd seen in Berkeley and would later understand what my stepmother was about to pull off and get away with my full family's consent, and to show how naive I was at the time, I didn't realize that (a) there was no will, (b) my father died at the hands of malpractice, and (c) his wife, Bess, was a world-renowned medical technologist who hired Melvin Belli and Singer to settle the case in 1981 for five hundred thousand dollars. Bessie would stage an elaborate party for all the family members including my ex-wife and kids and spent the rest of her life traveling and spending the money. Keep in mind the death certificate read no descendants based on what she told the authorities.

I was estranged from all these people and wouldn't put this whole joke on me together for twenty-nine years.

I thought about my father a lot when I returned, and Pete was telling me to improve my sales.

In the car business, the salesman is given three hundred dollars on the fifteenth of the month. This is considered a draw against commissions. The dealership takes their draw back on the thirtieth out of the commissions from your sales. I wasn't doing any real selling.

But two of the highlight experiences I had at Westwood AMC I will share.

I had a customer ask me about one of the Jeep Wagoneers we had in stock.

I recognized the actor Gary Collins right away and asked him if that was who he was, and we talked about the Wagoneer for a while. He thanked me for my time, took my business card, and told me that if he came back, he would ask for me.

Mr. Collins was a very handsome, pleasant, good-spirited, down-to-earth guy who had married Miss America Mary Ann Mobley and was deeply in love with his wife. I was a fan of a television series called the *Sixth Sense* that he was starring in, so I asked him esoteric questions to which he replied, "I don't know anything about the subject. I just follow the script." As he walked away, I realized that Mr. Collins had a presence and that he was a very nice man.

117

One afternoon, I was on the lot when across the lot walked Pam Grier, the actress, and a guy she was seeing named Greg Foster, who was an R&B artist. In my opinion, Pam Grier is as pretty today as she was back then. Her Cherokee Native American features gave her much added beauty. She would join the other African American actors in future legendary status, but that moment I would say that she was as pretty with no makeup and shorts as she was in the movies.

Pete called me into his office with a referral in his hand to see the sales manager at Central Chrysler/Plymouth on Central Avenue and Wilshire Boulevard. Pete told me that in his opinion I had lost my nerve or spark.

We hugged, and I used the AMC Hornet to pick up a 1978 Cordoba.

While I was happy to be driving a brand-new Cordoba, there were many other factors that were going to keep me from making me the money that I needed, like the fact that the Central Chrysler/ Plymouth was located on Wilshire Boulevard and Central Avenue, which was at that time a Korean neighborhood and the management was Korean. The Koreans that purchased their cars went directly to management for fleet discounts. This was meant that with eight black salesmen on staff and two whites, I had a situation that I'd never encountered before.

In 1978, Chrysler had just been redressed by a man named Lee Iacocca at the top, and because of a change in a size trend in cars at the time, the emphasis was on smaller cars and not Chrysler Imperials, Newports, Cordobas, Plymouth Furys, and other big used cars. Central Chrysler's inventory was full of cars that the public was not interested in, and to top it off I was trying to sell cars during the rainy season in Los Angeles, where it rained every day. On the home front, we relocated from the motel to a one-bedroom apartment on Arbor Vitae and Fir in Inglewood.

We were down the street from the Fabulous Forum, where the Lakers played.

An old friend of mine named Greta from St. Paul, Minnesota, who was living with her family in Carson, helped me by contacting her church, and within the same day, two members of the church came to our motel room and offered money. One named Doc Hester (God bless him) gave us permission to use his "retreat apartment" until we could do better.

The two boys slept on twin beds in the bedroom, and Marilyn and I slept on a single in the living room.

I wasn't selling many cars, but neither was anyone else at the dealership. We were all living off our draws of three hundred dollars. We drivers on the used car lot would sit and wait for hours waiting in the rain for potential customers. While we were waiting, we would talk and share stories.

One of the white salesmen was sharing stories about his stepfather abusing him and his mother. I could relate to his experience because of my background and what I'd seen growing up with my stepfather.

As he talked, we four listeners including Mike Bullock, who was employed by Motown and sold cars part-time, felt him when he was emoting about what his mother was going through. We all but Mike were shocked when he told us it was Lou Rawls, the singer.

Mike admitted that he had heard rumors about Lou and his abusiveness.

To show you how brainless I was at the time, I would go home and abuse my wife. Marilyn was emotionally spent from the entire experience of being with me and our guest?

She wanted to take the kids and go back to Minneapolis and her parents. Looking back, I probably felt that she was quitting on a shared situation without having tried to donate any effort toward helping by trying to work. In my own mind, I felt that we would prevail because I saw progress so far.

She wanted to quit, and from hindsight I should have said goodbye and moved on with my life.

Her aunt and many others had told me to send her back because she wasn't lifting a finger to help.

With all these factors involved, I had no reason to punch her in the arm. She bent over away from me, and I remember hitting her in the back.

I remember her saying, "Now I see what Roz saw!"

I probably apologized and told her that it wouldn't happen again because she stayed.

Mike Bullock came to work all enthused over a demo tape of a song about to be released by an artist named Jimmy Johnson from Philly.

We listened to Mike as he stated that they at Motown felt they had something. He put the cassette in, and we listened to both what would be called "Do You Love Me, Mary Jane" and "Bustin' Loose."

Mind you, we heard these songs on a tape recorder, and Mike told us his recording name would be Rick James. Mike turned out to be right.

CHAPTER
Thirty-One

Soon another management group took over Central Chrysler Plymouth and the culture changed from Korean to Polish and Dutch.

Larry Van Nostrum and Joe Stillinovich came in and promised big changes. He told the sales force to be patient a bit longer and we'd be making money.

They knew we were living off our draws, and some were depleting their savings. Our finance and insurance manager (Joe Klippenger) was taking a job somewhere else, but he asked me for my résumé. He saw my banking and sales background and gave me a lead for a finance and insurance manager in Orange County, and since he gave a two-week notice, he would give me a cram course in finance and insurance sales.

I set up an interview with Bob Price, who was the vice president of Bauer Buick in Costa Mesa in Orange County. Mr. Price at the time was thirty-five years old and one of the sharpest businessmen that I've met anywhere. After a two-hour interview, he hired me to be a salesman and gave me a week to get back there for the next training class to start.

This was about three weeks before Thanksgiving, and I had a child about to be born.

I requested to work at Bauer Buick along with twenty other new hires. I took a course provided by the Poorman Douglas Sales Institute in Seattle, Washington. As students, we studied every buying and selling phase of the automobile business since its inception and all the cars in the Buick line as well as all dimensions, appointments, classes, etc.

There were five hundred questions on the test, and out of those twenty that took the test I had the highest score. I answered every question right.

I got a five-hundred-dollar bonus for that, and considering the fact that all the other nineteen were under twenty-five-year-old college graduates, my twelve-year-old high school diploma at Washburn held up.

Soon it was time to hit the sales floor, and as well as I knew the information, I was not performing the way I should have. The Poorman Douglas team sales system was the most state-of-the-art complete automobile schooling I'd ever seen, and while it was intense, my problem was not with the system but with social cultural climate of being a black salesman in Orange County.

I never had the feeling that I was welcome at all.

Almost all the management was wealthy, and the sales force, although young, were very well-connected financially. I can now look back and honestly say that I was intimidated. No matter what my life experiences were at that point I was a thirty-year-old black man from Inglewood. There wasn't one person of color in the dealership besides me.

This was a first-class dealership on every level, and the customers that came in had no finance problem at all.

That Sunday, the twenty of us newbies hit the sales floor, and the lunch was catered in from a very expensive deli, so there would be no need for anyone on staff to leave this place.

I was overwhelmed by all the extravagance and class. I talked to a few customers, but I didn't sell anything. As bright as I was, I froze. Skip Gimbrone was my team leader and seemed nice but was of very little help because the general consensus was that I wouldn't last. Marilyn and the kids were days away from a brand-new baby to be born, and thank God for Greta, who donated all the baby bed and furniture we needed.

On one hand Marilyn and I had made progress, but I believe the struggle that she had to go through and my abusive acts had her trapped in California with a baby on the way.

I don't know what her plan was, but my focus was on selling cars and our survival.

CHAPTER
Thirty-Two

O n November 21, Marilyn called me at work to tell me it was time to take her to deliver the baby.

At around 8:00 p.m., I left the dealership and drove ninety miles per hour down the freeway hoping that I could draw a police escort but to no avail. I got home and picked up Marilyn and carried her down from second floor to the car and drove as fast as I could on the streets of Inglewood. Three blocks from the hospital, the police gave us an escort to the hospital named Martin Luther King. The nurses were ready at the ER with a wheelchair, and when Marilyn sat down, you could see the baby's head coming out.

In less than an hour Brandy Nicole Commodore was born, eight pounds and nine ounces.

At thirty years of age, my third child was born.

As I looked at her through the glass on the nursery window, I promised her that I would never leave her.

CHAPTER
Thirty-Three

Thanksgiving came, and at Christmas, my mother-in-law came and stayed for a week to see the baby and assist Marilyn. I was at work most of the time but really wasn't producing.

I was well-liked but not in sync with the system. I had a general manager named Doug Wisdom who intimidated everyone in the dealership for a number of reasons. First, he was so successful as a salesman and manager that he was promoted to general manager in a very short time and was the model.

Second, Doug was six feet and five inches and about three hundred pounds. He intimidated everyone but because of the all over environment, I felt that he was a bit more condescending toward me. He would play word games with me, and I would play word games back with him.

I talked to Bob Price about Doug just to cover for myself, and Bob would smooth things over and send me back to work. It all came to a point one afternoon when Doug called me into his office and browbeat me about my not understanding the system. I responded by letting him know that he might've intimidated everyone else with his size and Southern drawl, but I was not one bit afraid of him and would take him out if he just blinked at me wrong. I got up and went back to my desk and called a few of my customers.

After about fifteen minutes, Doug walked out on the sales floor, and with a smile on his face, he let me know that he had checked the phone records and that since I had been making too many calls home, it constituted theft of his time and that I was fired. I immediately went to Bob Price, and after explaining my side, Bob told me that I would do much better in the new dealership that they had just purchased in Torrance. He told me that I had to wait two months and reapply and take the course again to start. I agreed and got a ride home.

One of the most important experiences that I took with me was meeting Mr. Terrance Mills III and his wife at Bauer Buick one Sunday afternoon. I didn't sell him a car, but he told me that he and his wife liked me and he would get back to me soon. A couple of days later, he and his wife made a special trip back to give me two gifts. The first time I met them I told his wife that she smelled very good and asked what she was wearing. Her reply was that it was called Ciara. I told her that it was a wonderful smell. Mrs. Mills gave me a hundred-dollar bottle of Ciara for my wife. I'll never forget what Mr. Terrance Mills said to me. He said, "Bill, you have what it takes to be a great salesman, and I'd like to share something that I have found helpful for me." He handed me a book entitled *The Greatest Salesman in the World* by Og Mandino.

Mr. Mills told me that if he had been in the market for a car, he would have purchased one from me.

While I was waiting to go back to work, I read the book at least twenty times. My experience in Orange County was no different from working in Minnesota; the mentality was the same.

The call finally came from Bob Price, and I got on the bus from Inglewood to Torrance and interviewed with him. He explained to me that he felt that Torrance was a better fit for me, and this time there would be forty students.

Bay Buick had replaced Lions Buick that had been advertised as the largest in the world. Mr. Bauer already owned four dealerships in Southern California and three back in Harvey, Illinois, where he came from. Mr. Bauer owned condos near every dealership and was a man of great class.

I went to Bay Buick armed with the book Mr. Mills had given me. The book was about a man in the Far East who was given ten ancient scrolls of wisdom to recite three times per day and each for thirty days. I believed that I could become great.

When class started, there were forty college grads between the ages of twenty-two to twenty-eight years of age, and this time there was another black man in the class.

Once again, I was the top student with a perfect score and got another five hundred dollars.

We were divided into four teams of ten, and I hit the ground running.

My book said one scroll three times a day and recited the scroll's ancient affirmation.

I was using all ten scrolls and affirming five times a day. My aim was to be the top salesman at the end of the month. I worked thirteen hours per day and was going seven days a week and literally burned my system out. At the end of the month I had lost thirty pounds and was so sleep-deprived that I was almost hallucinating.

The pace was so intense that Bob Price brought five of his best salespeople from his Orange County dealership.

The pace that I had set and continue to sell at wiped out fifteen salespeople who were getting sick and dropping from exhaustion. I wasn't getting much sleep at night because I was literally using my mind over matter. I was convincing myself that I had to be the best for the entire black race. The first salesman of the month had to be a black man. I was so focused on selling and winning that I was burning the candle at both ends. I was up at 7:00 a.m. and working until 10:30 p.m., getting in at 11:00 p.m. and talking to Marilyn about the car business until 1:00 or 2:00 a.m. and burning myself out. I'm sure Marilyn could see all the signs of my coming apart and was probably saying to herself, "Here we go again."

CHAPTER
Thirty-Four

I won the sales contest, and the management could see the emotional and physical toll that the contest took on the sales force. There were people that had to be hospitalized, some had quit, and even though I had outsold everyone else, I had "burned the wheels off the racing car." My team manager Rick McNary pulled me aside, and as he handed me my check for five hundred dollars for winning the contest, he told me, "You're good, and starting Monday we'll show you how to work smarter and win again." He told me that in a very short time I'd be a team manager and that "the sky is the limit."

I went back to my office and called my dad in Minneapolis to share with him my accomplishment.

This call would change my life. After I told him my good news, I asked him how he was doing, and he said, "You mean you don't know?" I told him that I didn't, and that was when he told me that he was dying of cancer and that he only had about six months to live. When I look back on that moment, I think that for a combination of reasons, exhaustion, going from a super exhilarating feeling to the worst low, hearing that someone that I had great love for was leaving this world, I fell completely apart on the spot.

I let out a yell that startled everyone in the dealership. I just bawled and dropped the phone and was crying uncontrollably.

Mr. Bauer came out of his office and took me to his office and told of how he felt when he lost his father. He told me two things: First, he said, "You've got a million-dollar smile and use it only a hundred dollars' worth." The second thing he told me was that I was a great salesman and that I should go home for the weekend and get some rest. I drove home crying and was so distraught that

Marilyn called her parents back in Minneapolis, and within twen-ty-four hours my dad was on a plane to Los Angeles.

One of my friends, Ted Milan, drove us to the airport, and we picked up my dad and brought him to our place in Inglewood.

I was mentally gone but not so far gone that I didn't see him walk down the hall and plant a kiss on Marilyn's lips and give her a hug. I took a bath while the two of them discussed my mental state. When I came back, I could tell that they were treating me in a man-ner that people treat people that they feel are cuckoo or nuts.

I was in bad shape but not as bad as they thought. I realized that the two of them had control over me. By that I'm referring to my resisting what they felt was best for me in their own opinions. I sat that evening and talked with my dad after Marilyn and the kids were asleep. We went down memory lane.

I was reminding him of the two of us sitting in front of the television watching the finals of the nationals of the Golden Gloves in Chicago when we saw a skinny tall rangy kid, sixteen years old, from Louisville Kentucky come out of his corner and box. At the end of the third round, when the kid walked back to his corner, my dad said, "That kid will be a world champion someday."

That kid's name was Cassius Clay, and the rest is history. When I asked my dad what he saw that made him so sure, his response was "I don't know." I had a feeling. Soon we were in the living room up on our feet in boxing stances, and he threw semislow punches at me in combinations.

I never told him that I studied martial arts, and "sticky hands" practice prepared me to pick off his punches as they were coming out. Pretty soon he was throwing four- and five-punch combinations and I was just standing there with no effort parrying his shots.

Suddenly he stopped and, with a smile on his face, said, "Let me show you something." He put me in what Verne Gagne, a legendary champion wrestler, used to refer to as the sleeper hold.

So, he got me in this hold, and as he was talking to me. He was telling of the years he worked as a guard at the St. Cloud State Prison and that they taught him this. I was almost blacking out, and he was reminding me of a time when I was about six years old and he told me to watch his ears wiggle. I came closer, and then he burned me with his cigarette in his other hand. As I was blacking out, I told him to let go. His responded with "What?" I repeated, "Dad, let me go!" He responded with "What?" again. I repeated once more, "Dad, let me go." He let go, but he made his point.

His alcoholism had his weight down to 155 pounds, and I was about 160 pounds, but I was ready for bed and not very happy about what he had just done to me.

The next morning, I got up and came into the living room, and he had his bottle of Christian Brothers brandy sitting on the floor next to a glass of ice cubes. My thought was that it was ten in the morning as I went in the bathroom and closed the door.

What happened next is one of the strangest things that I've witnessed in my life.

I don't know what came over me, but when I opened up my mouth, my father's voice said, "Junior Wynn, first you fuck my wife, and now you want to fuck my son's wife, you motherfucker." I heard the voice, and it wasn't mine, but it must have scared everyone on the other side of the door. My dad immediately tried to force his way in, but I was sitting on the sink and using my legs and feet to barricade the door. I was telling him about all his abuse in the past, and my language was very salty.

Soon I hear a voice on the other side of the door telling me that it was the police and to come out immediately. When I came out, I was thrown to the floor and taken to Metropolitan State Hospital in shackles. This time I knew the drill and was back in three days. When I walked through the door, the first words out of my dad's mouth were "You tricked and conned those people." He was very angry.

My dad left in a couple more days. He had a wife and kids to get back to.

On the way to the airport, I asked him if there was anything, I could do for him.

His answer was that he wanted me to come home because he wanted me there in his last six months.

I made a mistake that would haunt me for many years. I gave him my word that I would go back.

He didn't believe me and told me so. I said, "Honest to God." He said he believed me because he knew that when I said honest to God, I would keep my promise.

CHAPTER
Thirty-Five

On Monday, I reported back to Bob Price at Bay Buick, and he grilled me about my state of mind and if I was on any drugs at the time. I noticed that after each question he would look down into an open drawer in his desk. About a month before, John Allen, the finance and insurance manager, was showing me an executive's catalogue of office supplies.

In the catalogue I saw a lie detector that you sit in the desk to use for interviews, where the green light shows for truth and the red light for a falsehood. Bob Price must've been looking at one of these devices because he told me he believed me and sent me back to work. I went back to my desk and sat down and just stared straight ahead processing. After about ten minutes, I got up and went to Mr. Bauer's office and told him what my dad requested.

Mr. Bauer told me, "If you stayed at Bay Buick, our program will make you successful, but you may one day regret not giving in to your dad's request. He raised you and came all the way to California to help you because of what he told you."

I went to one of the desk managers and told him why I had to leave and asked for a referral letter from the dealership.

He wrote it with a pure professional tone and stated that I was the top salesman out of forty salesmen. He signed it, dated it, and put his phone number on it. He hugged me and wished me good luck.

I went back home, and we made plans to leave.

I had a million mixed emotions and took all my chaos and put it on Marilyn, who set my friend Danny up to drive me to the nuthouse again while she took about $1,200 and had my friend Reggie drive her and the kids to LAX. Danny came to the house and actually told me that we were taking a ride and talked to me while he drove me to the state hospital.

When we got to the hospital we went inside to the desk, where he proceeded to try to commit me. The people asked me if I was aware of what was going on, and I told them that I was just coming in with him and that he'd asked me to go for a ride. Danny came unplugged when they told him that they didn't see anything wrong with me.

Danny cussed and yelled at me all the way to my house about my faking normalcy.

Yes, I was absolutely out of my mind, and in fairness, all the men involved were responding to whatever my wife was telling them and they only wanted to take me somewhere and discard me. I went in the apartment and called my dad and told him that I was ready to come back. He called back in about an hour and told me to just go to the airport and that the flight was already paid for.

I called Danny and asked for a ride to the airport, and when he arrived, I asked him to store the things in my apartment in his garage and that I'd pay for shipping later.

Danny dropped me off, and after our conversation he told me to keep my eyes open and remember that the general consensus was that Marilyn was my problem.

Once again, I was leaving California to go back to a wife and family and for the second time not as a hero. It was a case of the prodigal son returning.

CHAPTER
Thirty-Six

I caught a midnight flight and sat on that plane thinking about Gladys Knight's singing, "I'm leaving on a midnight train to Georgia."

I know that I had some unfinished business in Minnesota and that I would have a large network of people watching me.

I came to understand that I felt that I had an obligation to my dad to be there for him since he was there for me. My daughter Brandy was almost a year old, and this time I wasn't going to leave my child behind.

My plane landed at Minneapolis International Airport at 5:15 a.m., and my brother-in-law Butch was waiting for me at the upper deck when I walked out.

As he drove me to my family staying with Marilyn's parents, we made small talk and laughed until we landed at the duplex.

Butch was married to Marilyn's sister Connie, and they lived upstairs above my father and mother-in-law. Everyone was still in bed when we got there so I just went into Marilyn's bedroom and got into bed and went to sleep.

Later that day I called my Dad to tell him that I had landed. He seemed surprised, and I would find out later that he had set me up to stay with him and his family at his place.

The atmosphere at my in-laws' home seemed tense downstairs, so Marilyn and I went upstairs to visit Butch and Connie. We'd play card games and crack jokes and laugh and loosen the mood. By Monday morning, I was ready to seek employment. My dad's wife was working at a company called North Star Processed Potatoes and suggested we apply because there were always openings. Marilyn and

I rode a couple of buses to get there and went back home with two jobs.

Marilyn was not happy, and even though we had three children to take care of, she seemed resistant.

From hindsight I believe that Marilyn was in a state of post-traumatic stress from all she had been through with me.

I believe Marilyn was trying as hard as she could to let the bottom fall out of our relationship. It had certainly been a mistake, and now she was back at her parents' home with another child and a crazy husband. Marilyn and I boarded the bus to go to work that Wednesday. As we rode to work, her mood got darker and darker, and by the time we walked into the plant, she was no longer talking to me. I went into a locker room and put on my work clothes, and for the next four hours straight I spent my time shoveling rotten potatoes and putting them in a wheelbarrow and rolling the contents to a room to be extinguished.

I went by Marilyn, who was cutting the eyes out of the potatoes coming down a conveyer belt. She had safety glasses that were filling up with potato juice. She gave me a look that said, "This is all your fault."

The shift went quickly because we'd worked from 11:00 p.m. to 7:00 a.m. As we rode the bus back home wet and cold, Marilyn told me that she wasn't going back there anymore.

I was disheartened to think that she would quit on her family that quickly. My dad's wife had been working there for ten years and said that Marilyn should do whatever she could to feed those children.

I had never seen the red flags from 1975 to 1979, and I was so stupid that I couldn't see that it was indeed over. I went back to that potato plant and worked there for three more weeks while I looked for another job during the day.

I landed an assistant manager training position with a corporation called Big Wheel Auto Parts.

I rode the bus each morning for a couple of weeks until my father-in-law loaned me the spare car. I worked fifty hours per week for $250.

CHAPTER
Thirty-Seven

Marilyn was not looking for work under any circumstances, and it was not just becoming a problem; it had been a problem the entire time we'd been together. I was so stupid that I refused to see that she was no longer in a relationship with me.

My brother-in-law and I went for a ride, and that's when he confided in me the fact that everyone had been watching me for signs of mental illness since I got off of the plane because Marilyn had told them that I had been locked up in the state hospital indefinitely.

The fact that I showed up the next day and been the normal person they knew, they were confused. He said that Marilyn had a track record of lying, and he wanted me to be aware of what was going on.

He told me that the two of us were under a microscope because of the way she talked about me.

I admit that people were just curious, and when I look back at one of those first couple of years of social adjustment, I wasn't very mature. My in-laws were absolutely fair to me because they knew my background. They knew my biological parents and my stepfather's family. They knew what I was missing and gave me an unbelievable amount of patience and love. They were giving me more than enough fair treatment. The reality was that Marilyn had been through a nightmare in a relationship with me.

We had a daughter, but the love and respect were no longer there anymore. I had so many unresolved issues, and at that point I had not sat down and began the process of putting my life into perspective.

I had been going through each day existing without realizing how my behavior was affecting my surroundings.

I didn't have a clue. I was creating reasons for promoting my own self-pity parties. People listened out of respect, but I didn't realize that I was the problem. On one occasion, I had joined church because I needed help. The primary reason for attending the services was that you got into the Labor Union and got a construction job.

This came through my brother-in-law's friend. Tommy was a manager for a company known as Northern States Power Company.

I had been attending services for a while, and this particular Sunday morning I was sitting in the bathtub reading the Bible. My marriage was over, but I felt that Jesus was going to heal my marriage.

Marilyn came in the bathroom and accused me of wasting her father's hot water. I finished my bath, got dressed, walked into the kitchen where she was sitting at the kitchen table, and punched her right in the eye.

Her parents come back the next day, and it took a superhuman effort for my father-in-law to be fair to me.

No father wants to see his daughter with a black eye. I was so ashamed I stayed in the house for most of the Fourth of July. My brother-in-law was using all his composure, and his words to me were "I cannot judge you because I've been guilty of putting my hands on women in the past, but one day if this happens to your daughter, you cannot do anything."

CHAPTER
Thirty-Eight

I went to NSP to work and was issued a hard hat, goggles, and gloves. I reported to Curly, who gave me an air hose and told me that my job was to blow the dust out of these large generators.

As soon as he turned on what amounted to three hundred pounds of air pressure, I heard the pop in my ears, and I was deaf. I filled out an accident form and was sent to the University of Minnesota and had a battery of auditory tests. I went home and would suffer from post-traumatic stress syndrome for another thirty-five years and not know it. Instead of talking, I yelled everything.

People would talk to me, and I would act like I heard them, but I really didn't.

I got another construction job and moved into the YMCA and with a friend of mine.

I went to Marilyn's to see Brandy one Friday night and spent the weekend. Sunday morning came and Marilyn wanted me out in a very ugly way, and when I left and got in the car, I realized that I had left some overnight clothes behind. My stepson was laughing while he threw my belongings out of the second-story window.

I told him to tell his mother to come down to the door. Marilyn came down and was cussing. I lost it and put my fist through the glass, and a piece of glass cut her nose.

That act of domestic violence was a turning point in my life. Marilyn ran across the street, and my sister-in-law called the police and made a citizen's arrest. I was then in a squad car on my way downtown to jail. I was treated well because my last name was Commodore and my uncle was a sheriff, and so I became a novelty.

I asked them not to tell Reggie, but I knew they would. They even gave me a powder-blue princess phone to call and talk all night.

I called my mother and her husband, and they were trying to convince me that my marriage was over.

The next day, Monday, I went to court, and on my way down the hall toward court, Mary Starkey intercepted me, and after a few of her questions I was crying.

Mary explained the diversion program was called DAP (Domestic Abuse Project).

She said that if I attended thirteen weeks of anger management classes and committed no more acts of domestic violence for a year, my sentence of 180 days in jail would be avoided. I agreed, and when I walked out of the courtroom, my mother was standing there with my five-hundred-dollar bail money. She gave me a ride back to my car still parked at Marilyn's house and asked me to leave Marilyn and her family alone and go on with my life. My DAP classes began the next Wednesday, and a man named Corky Galloway was running the program. There were about fifteen other men in the class, and for me, it was a life-changing experience because it was academic to me and I took to it like a duck to water.

I learned about things like the honeymoon cycle and aspects of domestic violence that I never imagined existed.

I looked forward to my Wednesday classes and learned the mechanics of self-control. The thirteen weeks went by, and I was so impressed that I signed up for thirteen more.

CHAPTER
Thirty-Nine

I was adjusting to my new single lifestyle when a friend of mine had a birthday party for me at her place, and not many showed up, but it was all right with me because it was planned on short notice.

The last to arrive was John Williams. John was a special person and would change my life forever. I met him in the fall of 1966 when we were in college. We were both dating the same girl and didn't know it. My friend Wes, whom I was working at the bank with, invited me to a house party that he and his sisters were having. Wes knew that we were both dating his sister, and he also knew that I was dating my girlfriend Roz. Wes invited Roz and her brother Rockie just to see what would happen on the night of the party. On the night of the party, I was sitting with Wes's sister Sandy when John Williams and his friend Bud (McKinley Boston) came down the basement steps. John was a fullback for the University of Minnesota, and at that time he was about six feet and four inches tall, 230 pounds of muscle, and was good-looking to boot. The two of them were wearing their U of M lettermen's jackets proudly, and I could also see my girlfriend Roz and her brother right behind John and Bud. When Sandy got up to greet John and Bud, I went to greet Roz and her brother, and Wes got a good laugh out of this setup. John would go on to injure a hamstring on a forty-four-yard run. With his versatility, he reinvented himself and became an all-American guard and would go on to a ten-year all-pro guard and tackle for Baltimore Colts and Los Angeles Rams football teams.

When I was reintroduced to John in 1981 at my birthday party, he had retired from pro football and was now Dr. John Williams, DDS, a local dentist. We connected and began to hang out together.

Adele had dated John, and because she had been impressed by me, she told him good things about me. I liked John and respected him for his personality and the fact that for all his accomplishments he was extremely down to earth.

At the time John lived in Chaska, Minnesota, but would come by the apartment that I shared with my buddy Dwight Dean. John's vehicle broke down, and I had recently purchased a 1976 Buick Park Avenue Limited to go with my 1964 Dodge. I gave a set of keys to John and told him that the Park Avenue was fully covered with insurance.

He wanted to know what I was going to drive, and I told him the Dodge. I told him to get it back to me when his car was finished. John gave it back to me in about two weeks, and in return he scaled my gums after hours at a discount price and taught me oral hygiene.

I would visit John at his office after I got off work, and we'd talk and go back to my place or to his place in Chaska.

At that time, he was ending his marriage, and mine was on the rocks, so we were good company. We talked about our experiences in Los Angeles and what it meant to come back to Minneapolis. John had listened to me long enough to wonder why I was in construction as a laborer instead of business. He asked for my résumé and about a week later gave me a referral to interview at Allstate Insurance Company in Edina, Minnesota, with a man named Tom Sakal.

When I got there, the interview went surprisingly well, and Mr. Sakal offered me a job.

He explained to me that I would be sent to Chicago, Illinois, for four weeks of training at four hundred dollars per week and then brought back to Minnesota and that I'd been part of the program.

As I sat there, I thought about my daughter and my dead marriage and used the four hundred dollars as the excuse for turning down the position, saying to him that I was already making four hundred dollars per week. Mr. Sakal was disappointed and let me leave. At about 6:00 p.m., I got a call from John, and he was disappointed and let me know that Mr. Sakal was going to mentor me into a wonderful career in the insurance business. John explained to me that he and Tom Sakal had been teammates on the Minnesota

Gopher football team together and had earned all-American status in their respective positions. Tom was all-American as a linebacker and was captain of the 1967 Big Ten Championship Squad. Their relationship was strong enough that John could recommend me as a good candidate for a successful career in sales in the insurance industry. John was asking for a favor. I had the job and was more than qualified for the position.

For the second time in my life, my immaturity would cost me a career that would have been successful in the long run.

I had blown my opportunity with Bank of America and now this opportunity with Tom Sakal, and John was deeply disappointed and confused by my lack of judgment in this case.

I would never get another opportunity like this again. Tom Sakal would go on to become unbelievably successful in the insurance business, and I fumbled the ball.

John, being a friend, never kept reminding me of my lost opportunity, but he shook his head in amazement of my stupidity. John and I remained friends, and I would get laid off in the construction business and spend the winter of 1981 on unemployment and enjoy one of the coldest winters in Minnesota weather history from my home every day.

CHAPTER
Forty

I cannot forget 1981 as the year that I would learn to stop lying.

I would spend time with another friend Ron Sayers (his cousin was Gale Sayers, the hall of fame football running back). Ron and I had been through thick and thin together, and I had one problem—lying. I would talk to Ron on the phone, and he would ask me if I was going to drop by his business and visit with him. I would say yes and just blow him off and leave him waiting while I would go do something else. Ron got tired of this treatment and insisted that I drop by his shop for an important chat. When I got there, Ron informed me that he could no longer be friends with me because I didn't comprehend the value of the truth. Ron had tears in his eyes and began to cry. I cried and gave him my word that I would stop lying. This was my third life-changing experience of 1981, and I will always cherish Ron's talk with me because I realized Ron's words: "The truth will set you free."

Thirty-six years later and I still have not told a lie or lied by omission. Thank you, Ron Sayers.

CHAPTER
Forty-One

I would go visit John at his dentist office, and between patients we'd sit in the backroom and talk.

In late October, John brought me into his inner circle and came by my place with one of his friends whom I'll call Raymond. Raymond had been a pro boxer and was a large man like John, who at that time was about 290 pounds. Raymond was weighing about 240 pounds. They came by and introduced me to what was referred to as baseball.

This was not a sport and was in reality freebase. They had the utensils for smoking purified cocaine. They prepared the process of removing the impurities from the 97 percent pure "Peruvian flake" cocaine and placed the pure "rock" into a glass pipe and ignited it with a gas burner, and each of them took a hit and passed it to me for my turn. John gave me my hit and told me to go sit down on my couch and sit still while I held the hit in my lungs.

I took my hit, and upon exhaling heard the bells and whistles go off in my head as I experienced an emotional orgasm.

At the time I weighed about 175 pounds, and I was matching these two giants hit for hit. Soon I was sitting lotus style with a pair of headphones on my head enjoying Santana music like never before. I kept taking my turn and never realized that these guys were much bigger and could consume more volume than I could, but to be honest I was in the "twilight zone" and didn't know it. I looked over at my pipe mates, and the two of them were crawling on the floor in the kitchen looking for white granules to put in the pipe. When I asked them why they were crawling around on the kitchen floor, I was told that everyone "trips" different.

Since my roommate worked nights as a fireman and wasn't around, we three played "baseball" each night, and I was in a different universe. These guys were pros at this "sport," and I was becoming a rookie.

I had heard John Bellucci talking about "baseball" on *Saturday Night Live* but didn't understand the reference at the time.

In the seventies, freebase had become the elite drug of the wealthy, and soon the poor would be introduced to crack, which was far more damaging to the body and mind.

In Hollywood, freebase and something called locker room would be the two most talked about recreational drugs. My friend Joey (Italian high roller) told me of how he and his women would use it to intensify their orgasms.

In truth, locker room was amyl nitrate, a heart recusant for someone having an angina attack. It works by relaxing blood vessels and increasing the supply of blood and oxygen to the heart while reducing its workload. I had tried it at a party in Hollywood Hills with my Italian friend Pete and his wife. I was with Judy at the time, and Pete had a tray of what seemed like all the drugs to be sampled while we consumed good wine as couples. Pete suggested the amyl nitrate that was inside a One a Day vitamin bottle. I inhaled the substance and sat back for what seemed like an hour and went to a place that I still haven't figured out to this day. I regained consciousness and was told that I had been out for only two minutes.

I was so immature I did not take the time to evaluate what I was participating in would affect my thinking process in the future.

John was sharing with me, and I was accepting a gratuity in friendship without a perspective.

I enjoyed the friendship and special way he treated me. He was one of the greatest offensive tackles in the history of football, yet he had a way of treating me in a special way. John and I would have a trusting friendship that would last thirty more years.

We freebased through one of the coldest subzero winters in Minnesota history, and I remember being at his home in Chaska and watching the entire Superbowl game, Because of our playing "baseball," I still don't remember who played in the 1982 game to this day.

By the end of January, I had become unstable and to be honest insane. My family and friends could see by my behavior that I was as mad as a March hare.

I was blacking out and acting in a very bizarre manner. I had been to Crazyville before and come back, but this time I was a mess, to say the least.

On one occasion, I called my grandmother Commodore at 3:00 a.m. and asked her to help me recite the Lord's Prayer. She and I said it at least thirty or forty times before she told me to get some sleep. In about two days my uncle called me from Denver asking me if I was on cocaine. I asked him why he was asking me. His response was that nobody calls an eighty-year-old woman at three in the morning to rehearse the Lord's Prayer forty times. He asked me to call her at a time when she was going through the day.

CHAPTER
Forty-Two

Two days later, on a January night around 2:00 a.m., I was so missing my three-year-old daughter that I put my coat on and ran about two miles in two below zero weather to my in-laws back door and hit the back window, which was now plexiglass, with my fist to break in and see my child.

My father-in-law came to the back door with a pump shotgun and asked, "Who is it?"

I lowered my voice to sound similar to my brother-in-law's voice and responded with "It's Chuck." My father-in-law opened the door, and when he saw who it was, he told me to go home and call my mother. I left his place and ran a couple of blocks headed to my brother-in-law's house, but I never made it because I passed out in a snowdrift on Thirty-Sixth and Nicollet Avenue South.

When I woke up, I was in the Hennepin County Crisis Center.

I was drugged up and on seventy-two-hour hold. I could have died, but God wasn't finished with my story. I had enough presence to begin drinking large amounts of hot water and exercising to drain the drugs out of my system.

In two days, I was back to earth realizing what I'd gotten myself into. My reality came back when I recognized one of the other patients from childhood. I walked up to him and said, "Billy Whiteside, how are you?"

Whatever drug he was on he remembered me, and we talked about high school and the gang called the Suprees. After about an hour, he excused himself and went back to the window that he had been looking out of, and I never saw him again. I thought to myself, "What is Billy doing here? There's nothing wrong with him."

The next day my seventy-two-hour hold was lifted, and my roommate came and got me and balled me out for being in a nuthouse when there was nothing wrong with me.

Dwight knew that I'd been freebasing and told me to get some rest. I was so messed up that I didn't comprehend that the word had spread about my mental illness throughout my families, friends, and everyone that knew me.

My roommate tried as hard as he could to stabilize my thought process and was on the phone trying to get help for me.

The last straw came when I called 911 and told the operator that I was having a heart attack.

In minutes a team of people came into the apartment and hooked me up with wires, and with a disgusted look on their faces, they looked at each other, packed up, and left without saying a word.

I was so embarrassed. Right behind them my fireman roommate came in and balled me out for calling them. He had heard the call at the fire station and rushed over.

Dwight had had enough and called my closest friend Paula and asked her to come over. She came over, and they talked while I was taking a bath. When I came back out, Paula had already loaded my belongings in her car and drove us to her townhouse in Maplewood.

I found out years later that Dwight had told Paula that I was secretly in love with her but wouldn't act on it because of her relationship with Orville Shannon, our childhood friend.

When Paula and I got to her townhouse, I moved into her son's bedroom. Her son was living with his father.

We sat down at the dining room table and had a long talk. Paula was my wife's best friend and yet because of what Marilyn was purposely doing to me gave the reason to develop a friendship with me. It was out of her compassion for me that was the foundation of our friendship.

Marilyn in a conversation with Paula referred to me as her ticket out of Minnesota. She lost respect for Marilyn because of the way it came across.

We sat at the table, and I admitted to her that I was still suffering the effects of freebasing cocaine to the excess. My mind was all over the place, and Paula watched over me at night and would tell me when I was tripping from the withdrawal of the drugs. She pointed out my bizarre behavior to me and made me look at it, and we would both laugh.

CHAPTER

Forty-Three

Over the next thirty days, I healed and regained my perspective. At some point I proposed to Paula, and she accepted.

I moved into her bedroom, and we were a couple. I met her parents, and her father knew not only my father but my mother and her family also. He had gone to Lakeville Jr. College with my father and knew who I was.

I liked him right away. He was an aristocrat and as brilliant a man as I have ever met. Talking to Talmage Carey Jr. to me was like having conversations with a master.

I was sitting with royalty, and the wisdom of this man was unsurmountable. He had a confidence and presence that I can feel every time I remember him. He was close friends with the Rothchild family and Senator Mondale, among many others. Paula had told him that I was intelligent, so he wanted to meet me.

CHAPTER
Forty-Four

March came, and I had recovered enough to seek employment, so I looked in the ads and saw a position as a meter reader available.

I went downtown and filled out an application and waited a week, and when no call came, I called and got a woman's name in the personnel department. I called and talked to her every afternoon for about two weeks, and sometimes our conversations would last at least fifteen minutes to a half an hour.

I believe she became curious enough to call me in for an interview.

I went in for the interview and arrived about fifteen minutes before my appointment, and as I was sitting at her desk, I saw her coming back from lunch with another woman. She was wearing a skirt too short for her age and no nylons.

She introduced herself, and I noticed that her blouse was too low-cut for me to be comfortable.

She kept getting up from her chair and bending over forward toward me as she pointed out something on my application. I avoided looking and tried to focus my eyes on the paperwork. I got the job, and yet I wondered if the woman was really making a pass at me. My suspicions were confirmed when another meter reader friend came out to our house, and at the dining room table, I asked Kemit if he had experienced an interview like mine.

Kemit's response was that he had and admitted the he had gone to the woman's house and "hosed" her a few times.

My buddy John and Ron would come out and visit Paula and I on many occasions. I believe it was because of Paula's beauty. Paula was one of the prettiest women I've ever known. Today they call women like her trophy women. You get great credibility just walking around with her.

Paula and I were a perfect match, and yet one evening she sat me down at the dining room table and announced that we were breaking up as a couple.

Paula and I hadn't had a bad moment, but she felt guilty about being Marilyn's friend and being with me.

I didn't object in any way and moved back into her son's bedroom. We became soul mates on a spirit level and lived together another year.

Our friends knew we were roommates, and we became a magnet.

CHAPTER
Forty-Five

B y spring of 1983, I got a call from my cousin Phil, who was in town for his mother's funeral.

He asked me to stay in his mother's house and pretty much guard his sister Tracy and her newborn girl from her boyfriend Leon. I went over after work for a few days, and it was an experience because I really hadn't spent any time with these cousins.

Growing up, their mother was my mother's first cousin, which meant that Phil and his sisters were really my second cousins even though I always called their mother my Aunt Doris. The short experience was good because even though we grew up only six blocks from each other I only saw them on a rare occasion.

I spent so much time with them that Paula asked me to move out.

It wasn't that I had overstayed my welcome; it was because I was at Paula's until I got my wits together.

When I look back on it, it was a poor decision on my part, and in three months it was time to go.

One moment to remember was the fact that in a conversation with Tracy, Prince came up, and I asked about him being a relative. She then asked me if I knew Skipper, to which I said no. I didn't even know that there was another Skipper in the family. I called my mother and asked why I never met him. She blew me off with some stuff about him being ten years younger than me, so I forgot about it. This was 1983, and Prince was topping the record charts, but I was a jazz lover, and his version of crossover music didn't appeal to me very much.

I had lived in Hollywood and seen enough Hollywood exploitation and felt that Warner Brothers was marketing sex. People outside

Minneapolis don't realize that in the 1960s Minneapolis expressed a crossover style of pop and R&B music. This music was influenced by a street gang called the Suprees. Harold Boudreaux, who was probably one of the most talented all-around athletes in Minnesota state history, was also the leader of the gang.

The only other all-around talent on Harold's level was, in my opinion, David Winfield from St. Paul Central High School, a few years after Harold graduated in 1965. Harold was a magnet with a charisma like no one that ever lived before him or since. He formed the Suprees gang, and it was the only interracial gang in the state.

Though we were only high school kids, we dated interracially, and it drove the parents crazy. Harold lived at 4201 Fourth Avenue South on the corner, and on any given weekend day, the row of Mercedes, BMW's, Corvettes, and Jaguars filling Harold's side of the street was many, obvious, and long. Some of the most beautiful girls came by to see Harold, and Mrs. Boudreaux was more than accommodating to everyone. From 1963 to 1966, the metropolitan area saw a fusion of cultures mixing like no other time in history.

Prince witnessed this cultural explosion, and it influenced his music to a great degree. The entire world enjoyed a style that our ancestors would've never believed would ever happen.

CHAPTER
Forty-Six

By fall, my mother's husband told me about an opportunity to become an owner operator in the taxicab business with a company named Town Taxi.

I went to northeast Minneapolis and got interviewed and on a handshake stepped into a 1979 Chrysler LeBaron Taxi and began driving and making payments.

I had a good reputation from a couple of previous times working for Southwest and Suburban Taxi. In 1983, there were a hundred drivers in the company, and yet there were only four drivers that were black. I had been a businessman almost my entire adult life, but at Town Taxi you could feel the racism and white superiority. The cab business hadn't changed in eleven years from a social standpoint, and I had an attitude about the racist environment and a chip on both shoulders.

I had no problem relating with the customers in their suburbs, but some of the drivers that were driving when I left Southwest Taxi to go to California were still in the business and remembered me. Yet I was a bit more experienced about people than most of them because their only experience was Minnesota. I look back now and realize that I was combative when presented with any form of racism on any level.

Minnesota Northern European men like to give you shit. It opens the door to subliminal racism.

I had had about twenty-six weeks of anger management tools under my belt, but it was to no avail when it came to racist males.

The taxicab they sold me had many problems, and they kept me in their shop. I wasn't happy.

Every time I was told that the cab was fixed, it would break down within two days, and I didn't see anything funny about it and let them know it. I was berating the poor mechanic, who was the business manager's son. On many occasions I yelled at him until he was in tears, and I dared anyone else to say anything to me.

I was angry and had many unresolved issues, and most people felt by my behavior was so volatile that I would snap and commit bodily harm, but I knew my boundaries.

In all my years of employment, I never put my hands on anyone. I'll admit to yelling when I needed to, but I wasn't a docile black man staying in his place.

My mother's husband had a reputation for being an older dignified gentleman, and I was seen as a rebel.

CHAPTER
Forty-Seven

It was around this time when my friend Wes, who was a prolific historian, began teaching me history. I began studying Egypt and pre-Egypt called Kemet. I learned that Herodotus studied in Kemet and recreated history under the Greek concept of something called Egypt.

Kemet means "black land," and Kemet Nu means black people. The word Egypt represents "New World Order" and means "Temple of the of the soul of Ptah." *Kemistry* means "black science." Now we see the word *chemistry* and we are not aware of the origin from black people.

I studied John Henrik Clark, Dr. Ben Jochannan, Dr. Charles Finch, Ashra Kwesi, Diop, and a host of masters that had gone to Egypt and studied and gone on tours to see the real civilization story. Although if one reads Albert Churchward, Gerald Massey, George Carey, and *The World's Sixteen Crucified Saviors* by Reeves, you balance and validate the black historians with Northern Europeans who funneled their works and supported something termed Freemasonry.

I began to expand my consciousness, but at the same time I was hurt and angry that the black truth had been whitewashed by Europeans. As I grew on an intellectual level, I began to see discrimination and racism from a new perspective.

I tried to talk to my civil rights-oriented mother, and she had no point of reference to comprehend the truth.

My family felt that my conversation only reaffirmed their already existing belief that I was indeed insane.

CHAPTER
Forty-Eight

In the spring of 1984, I met Sandy Johnson on a blind date set up by her sister Paula Green.

I called her on Valentine's day, February 14, and asked her out. She declined that evening, but a few days later she invited me to her father's house, where she had been staying while she was in town from Texas. Her sports car had broken down, and she was in the process of getting it fixed.

When she answered the door, I looked and thought to myself, "She's pretty." I went in, and we clicked right away and talked for a few hours. Sandy was born in Bagley, Minnesota, but lived with her mother on the Red Lake Reservation. She was ^{15}/16 Ojibwe and ^{1}/16 French Indian. Her mother gave her and her brother Brian up for adoption to Marvin and Lexi Johnson.

Marvin was from Wichita Kansas and Lexi was from Alabama. Marvin was a pilot for Republic Airlines for thirty plus years until they merged with Northwest Airlines. Marvin was a wonderful human being who would adopt five or six other orphans and raise them.

In 1984 when I met Sandy, she and Brian were the only ones left sharing the home with Marvin.

Sandy went to high school at Roosevelt, and her mother Lexi was distraught by Sandy's insistence on bringing black girls home.

Being of Southern roots Lexi felt that Sandy was acting in an unacceptable way and put so much social pressure on Sandy that Sandy was hospitalized with Bell's palsy.

When Sandy returned home, Lexi began the pressure, and Marvin stepped in and defended his daughter's right to pick her friends. Lexi made the mistake of challenging Marvin to choose between his wife and daughter.

Marvin stood by his convictions. I admire a man like Marvin for upholding what was right. Sandy had been in a relationship before me for seven years with an abusive male named Sonny.

When I met her, he was still in the picture, but I had learned a long, long time ago in the streets you have the game called cop and blow. It means that in most cases when you meet a woman, she has had a relationship or two before you met her. Most men don't want to accept reality when their time is up. So, when you come home and another "mule is kicking in your stall," you accept it graciously as being all a part of the "game" of male and female.

When Sonny saw me, he made two mistakes. He called me an old man, and at that time I was rock hard. I had an overwhelming amount of issues to take out on someone. I moved in with Sandy, and it only took a few weeks to realize that Sandy was lightning fast. Sandy had been in the game and lived in downtown Manhattan and moved around enough to be razor sharp when it came to people, period.

Sandy was Ojibwe, but the $1/16$ French Indian was just enough to make her a chameleon. Depending on her hairdo she could be Mexican, Latino, Puerto Rican, mixed black and white. This means she could go into any environment and blend in. Multitalented and quicksilver at the same time. Sandy wasn't working, so I had her riding with me while I drove cab. She was so pretty that none of the customers complained.

My mother rode with her husband when they met, and it resulted in the first and only black-owned cab company in St. Paul, Minnesota, history.

I didn't want to live in the city anymore, and my friend told Sonny that I was not one to mess with, so he left me alone. I never saw him again with the exception of a funeral for Sandy's younger half brother from her mother's second husband. He saw me and left me alone.

I sent Sandy to look for apartments in Bloomington with her father's second car while I was at work.

In Minnesota, in the case of an interracial relationship, the non-black applies for both and the black shows up on moving days. We moved to 10640 Brunswick Avenue in southwest Bloomington and lived in a very nice suburban environment. Eventually Sandy got a part-time job at The Coat Company in Loehmann's Plaza Shopping Center in Bloomington.

Sandy sold coats and was very good with people. I drove cab twelve to sixteen hours per day, and with her income and mine, her father paid a portion or the full month's rent. After a few months he could see that I was working sixty to seventy hours per week, so he helped us.

Sandy and I got along well, but I had a lot of issues and a lot of demons I was fighting. I believe that I actually had a death wish because on many occasions at Town Taxi, I had blown up many times and acted like I was about to do bodily harm, and because I didn't touch anyone, my acts of verbal abuse were tolerated because they were seen as verbal tirades instead of what they were—*verbal abuse in a work environment.*

In the beginning of our relationship, I only displayed abusive behavior outside our relationship with other males.

CHAPTER
Forty-Nine

My experience in the taxi industry in the suburban companies that I worked for were almost 90 percent positive. I was a businessman when I entered the taxi business with an impressive résumé in 1971, so my reentrance in 1983 gave me more people skills that were international (thank you, California). The owners of three of the companies not only knew me but my mother and stepfather and our reputation. The owners of three of the outfits that I drove for knew that my family established St. Paul Taxi, and those connected knew that it would have expanded and become a success had it not been for an honorable man named Jeno Paulucci.

The owners of these companies also knew the political power that it took to establish the first and only black-owned taxi company serving the St. Paul suburbs and city.

The final reason that I was able to have a few privileges was because I paid all my dues and never worked for any of their companies and never left any company owing anything.

My outbursts were almost always reacting to issues relating to racism and white supremacy.

Sandy felt safe with me, and we built a solid relationship. Sandy was a head turner, so many men openly flirted with her almost everywhere we went. I have never been jealous of another man talking to my woman because I understood cop and blow.

CHAPTER

Fifty

In 1984, one afternoon I got a cab order to go to the Excel Inn in Bloomington and pick up Mr. Atlas in the lobby.

I pulled up, and I went in. Standing there was the most muscular man I've ever seen in person before. He gets in my backseat and fills it up entirely to the degree that I cannot see out of my rear window. Tony Atlas, in 1984, when I met him, was 275 pounds and stood six feet and three inches in height and was sculpted muscle head to toe.

I took him to the Elite Gym at Ninety-Second and Lyndale, and he gave me a time to pick him up.

I was a wrestling fan from the time I had polio and was in an iron lung. Verne Gagne came to visit me and gave my grandfather a free pass to attend any professional wrestling event in Minneapolis or St. Paul, Minnesota. I was at a wrestling match at the Minneapolis Auditorium when I collapsed and had to be taken to the general hospital from the onset of polio. I remember that the loud noise of the crowd and seeing blood triggered a memory of one of my mother's beatings in an argument with my father that sent me to a hospital named St. Barnabas.

I literally grew up with AWA Wrestling.

So when I met Tony Atlas, I knew who he was. I remembered *Wrestling Revue* displaying a picture and an article when Tony Atlas and Rocky Johnson (Dwayne's dad) won the WWWF Tag Team Championship.

Before I left Inglewood, California, a brand-new gym opened called the Continental Gym. The owner was Mr. Universe Earl Maynard, who had been an outstanding wrestler and tag team champion with a man named Dory Dixon. Tony was leaner and larger than both of these wrestlers. Mr. Maynard was about to train me, and I had given him a deposit of one month's fee for training me. Mr. Maynard sold me when he told me that he took Christopher Reeve when he weighed 150 pounds and trained him into the superhero Superman we saw on the screen. Two weeks later I was in Minnesota with yet another lost opportunity. Tony knew all the people that I talked about. I dropped him off, and he invited me in, then I spent the rest of the afternoon talking wrestling. Tony was in town wrestling for Verne Gagne's promotion.

CHAPTER
Fifty-One

I had seen him perform on television and seen his interview. I bluntly told him that I objected to his interview style in regard to too many "yes, sirs" and "no, sirs" in his dialogue for the black audience to be attracted enough to want to pay money to watch his shows. I told him about Bearcat Wright and the dignified way that he handled himself, and Bearcat was the real deal in the fifties and sixties.

What I had said to Tony specifically was that he needed a gimmick beyond "yes, sir" and "no, sir." I told him, as an example, to put on a Superman outfit and become black Superman.

I smile because in the early nineties, Tony literally became the black Superman character I suggested in 1984. My brother-in-law had seen a show on cable TV that bounced around the country showing the indies or independent promotions and had seen Tony come out of the locker room of a high school gymnasium. This was a man that had wrestled in front of sold-out crowds at Madison Square Garden.

Most impressive was his talent for painting. Tony showed me some of his pieces, and he was good. His artwork was signed by Tony White.

Tony was born in Roanoke, Virginia, on April 23, 1954, which means that when I met him in 1984, he was thirty years old. I believe that he thought that I was a groupie instead of the thirty-six-year-old that I was at the time we were talking. When I told my girlfriend who I was talking to, she insisted that I take her to meet him, which I did. I called the desk at the motel, they rang his room, and he said come on over. When we got there, he came out from his room with no shirt on, which was imposing because this young man was ripped.

My woman was Ojibwe, so when he inquired as to her heritage and she told him what she was, he pulled out his Thunderbird from around his neck and revealed his Cherokee roots. I was amused by his bonding attempts and the way he kept flexing his pecs to impress her. I remembered thinking to myself, "I could punch this man as hard as I could, and he would just laugh at me." My woman was smiling and blushing at his obvious subliminal advances. He was referring to me as son. I was born May 20, 1948, so I could have informed him that I was his senior, but since we were both Taurus males, I chose to take the lower road and watch the show.

Tony didn't smoke cigarettes, but he chewed tobacco and liked to put cocaine on the end of the KOOL cigarette and smoke it. He ran out of "girl" and felt comfortable enough to ask me if I could get him a "piece."

I told him I could, and he gave me fifty dollars to score him a piece. He told me he only risked fifty dollars so that he wouldn't be taken advantage of.

Sandy and I went to an associate's residence in Richfield, and when I told him who it was for, he was excited and said he had seen Tony on television. I took the piece back to Tony's motel, and after three trips my associate gave me his phone number for Tony to have access anytime.

Tony told me that he had sparred with Big George Foreman in the past, and I told him I'd seen him and George in a picture. I told him how I'd been introduced to George by Adrianne Calhoun when we with my friend Ron Sayers and I were coming out of the Gopher Theater in downtown Minneapolis and how George, who was also younger than me, had not even looked at us and just impersonated Sonny Liston. I was feeling slighted by George and told my friend Ron that he had disrespected us. Ron told me, "You can whip George, he ain't so big." In about a year and a half I would watch George bounce Joe Frazier around the ring like a child. So much for whipping George.

Tony did business with my associate directly, and when my name came up, he told Tony that I was a faggot and could be validated by my cousin Phil True, his ex-brother-in-law. The next time

I saw Tony I had shaved my moustache off, and Tony told me that I looked like a pussy, as per my associate's declaration.

I saw Tony a few times, and when he made the switch from the AWA back to the WWWF, he told me that he was on the card at the Bloomington Metropolitan Sports Center wrestling Jesse (the Body) Ventura. There was some bad blood between them because Tony said that Jesse got his physique from Decca and had gotten sick.

Tony didn't have much respect for Hulk Hogan for his use of Decca to get his build. Superstar Billy Graham influenced many wrestlers with his imposing physique, among others Ken Patera.

Sandy and I attended the card at the Met, and I cannot speak for Hulk, but Jesse was a straight-up brother, and because of his friendship with Danny Carpenter, and Gary Hines and family was to be given street cred in the neighborhood. A woman named June who was in my cab in later years would describe Jesse (Jim Janos) throwing a pass to Danny Carpenter at a homecoming game at Roosevelt to win the game. June had been a cheerleader on the sidelines.

So Jesse and him wrestled for about fifteen minutes, and it was "time to go home." Jessie rolled Tony up for the pin and pulled his tights down giving the audience a "moon" with his ass out and rolled Tony onto his side after the pin so that Tony would have a difficult time pulling his pants back up.

I never saw Tony again, and I'm sure he left town. Vince McMahon would remove all of Verne Gagne's stable of stars from him.

Sandy would come home one night and tell me that she was pregnant, to which I responded in a very negative way. I had been fighting my own personal demons, one being the fact that my ex-wife wouldn't let me see my son and daughter. My family supported this act and I wasn't looking at my abusive past with Rosalind as the reason was that I was immersed in self-pity. Roz's father had told me in 1971 that he would take my children and family and friends away forever.

When Sandy told me of the possibility of her pregnancy, I wasn't very supportive at all and hurled a phone at her, missing by inches, yelling about not wanting to lose another. So much for my DAP training. To top it off, she was never really pregnant; it was a test.

Sandy had told me early in our relationship that she couldn't have children, so she never got pregnant, and the subject never came up again. I needed additional therapy and didn't realize it. I was so arrogant, insecure, and angry. Sandy called me one night late in the night and wouldn't tell me where she was, so in my arrogance I told her if she couldn't tell me where she was, then stay out there. Sandy in her own subconscious way had convinced me to straighten my hair and grow my beard out. I was so unconscious that I didn't realize that she had transformed my clean-cut looks into a thug-like-looking pimp character like her previous abusive Sonny.

I had become a hard-core-looking angry black man with a massive chip on my shoulder. When I met Sandy, I was about 170 pounds, and when she got through changing me, I looked pimpish. I was unconsciously feeding into her abandonment issues and didn't realize the damage that I was doing to her psyche.

I had a dual personality, and when I wasn't raving, I was loving and caring. Sandy was a very spiritual woman that was seeing through my hard-core displays of anger and tried to relate to the good in me.

I even had a psychic reader named Jeanette Cotton, who was extraordinarily accurate, so I knew what Sandy was feeling. I had an extremely Dr. Jekyll-Mr. Hyde personality, wherein I would put Sandy out and in remorse desperately look for her once she was gone. In 1985, I left Town Taxi and bought a taxi from the owner of Suburban Taxi and took my maladjusted-ass mind and body to a new environment.

CHAPTER
Fifty-Two

When I met the owner, I reminded him that I met him originally at my girlfriend's house in 1966 when he came downstairs with her brother Erick and was introduced to me. He was going to Catholic school with Erick, and they hung out together.

Gary sold me and an old friend of mine, who had recently been released from prison, taxis, and we got started with the company as drivers. When the letterman came to put the company logo on the side of our cars, I asked him to put my name, Skip, on each side front door, and I was the only driver with his name painted on the side.

I was a seasoned driver, yet I was judged by the company for my abusive behavior at Town Taxi, and my reputation for always paying my dues (company balance) came with me. I never had any problems with customers, but I was very verbally abusive when it came to being treated in a racist manner.

In one instance I was working late one night when a dispatcher named Hank Brown called my cab number on the radio system (which was voice dispatching in those days): "Number ninety, I can't see you in the dark, so smile so I can see you."

All the other drivers who may have been out working and listening probably got a good laugh on me. I didn't respond and turned my radio off and drove home. The next day I went to talk to the owner in his office and told him of the incident.

Gary assured me that that was not a reflection of what he and his company represented and that Hank Brown's dispatching shift started at 3:00 p.m. and that if I showed up twenty minutes early, I could express myself.

At 2:30 p.m., I went to the parking lot with two black drivers as witnesses since Suburban Taxi in those days was at Ninety-

Fourth and Humboldt in a business district only six blocks from the Bloomington Police Station. I know if anything uncontrollable happened, Gary would have someone call on me, and a squad would be on the premises immediately and that I would be the one going to jail. I had my friend Chester bring his gun with him in case I needed to show that I meant business. This was in 1985, and years later O. J. Simpson would go to prison in Las Vegas for creating the same illusion.

At 2:30 p.m., when Chester and I arrived, it wasn't raining anymore, and since the parking lot was dirt, there were mud puddles everywhere. At 2:45 p.m., Hank drove up to start his shift, and as he got out of his driver's side of the car, I was standing there. When he got out of his car with an arm full of books, I knocked them down into the mud puddles and told him that he was not going into work today and reminded him of his racist remark the previous evening and let him know that I was there to kick his ass for him.

Now mind you that at the time I was "pumping iron" (lifting weights) every day and weighed 185 pounds and stood in front of him with my hair straightened and combed straight back, resting on my shoulders player style, and with a full beard. I told him to "bring it" and went into a kung fu stance.

Hank stood six feet and two inches and was well over two hundred pounds, but I had a death wish. Hank did nothing and was pleading for me not to fight him, and I began berating him and creating a verbal illusion that in any second, I would strike him.

I could see Gary and his staff standing in the plate glass window watching the show, waiting for this angry black man screaming abuse at their dispatcher. Pretty soon all the doors of the businesses on the block had opened and everyone was standing outside witnessing my loud tirade. Hank kept telling me that he was late for his shift, to which I told him that he wasn't going to work that day and that he was going to get his ass handed to him. I told Hank to swing at me, so the result would be self-defense. I was out of my mind in anger but was smart enough not to touch him.

At 3:30 p.m., Gary told his business manager Mark Muldoon to come out and let me know that my twenty minutes was up and he had to have his dispatcher working. I had made my point to Hank and left an indelible mark on all 125 drivers and staff not to treat me in any type of racist manner. In the words of Steve Martin, "I was a wild and crazy guy."

CHAPTER
Fifty-Three

My over-the-top anger wasn't limited to the cab business but to the support and collections department in Hennepin County, who wanted child support for my son Bobby and daughter Lynnette.

When they called my home phone, I would tell them that I wasn't paying for children I wasn't able to see. They couldn't garnish my wages because I was an independent contractor and wasn't making any money after expenses (which was the truth).

Their response was that I had to take care of that separate matter in another part of their system. I told them that I wasn't paying for children I wasn't allowed to see and that it was their problem. No one wanted to hear my ranting, and they would leave me alone for a while until a new worker would call and it would start all over again. This was in the days before they passed a law in Minnesota where they could suspend your driver's license for unpaid child support.

I was out of control, and my mate and her father were aware of my core emotional problems. I believe that Sandy shared my childhood family issues with Marvin (her father). When she combined my childhood issues with issues regarding my ex-wives over my having a legitimate relationship with my children along with the racism that I was experiencing in the taxi industry, I truly believed that Marvin understood since he had dealt with these issues raising her and her brother Brian.

It was during this period when Sandy would go to my instructor at DAP Corkey Galloway and have him make contact with me for additional counseling. Corkey and I sat down and met about six times, and because he knew my family on the Commodore side, we discussed everything but my personal emotional issues. Corkey, in his own frustration, dismissed me. It was also during this period when

Sandy and I got married, and when my grandmother Guy discovered Sandy's native American heritage, a family secret was divulged. My Grandfather was 100 percent Cherokee from Kansas.

Joseph Edward Aitkin—when I asked her about him, she told me of her working in housekeeping at the Curtis Hotel and he as a doorman, and one day they found a room to conceive my father.

When my father was born, Joe, who was going back and forth to Kansas seeing his wife and children, was standing at his post at the door along with a man named Robert Wynn Sr. when a "godfather" ascended the steps and with his security around him uttered the command, "Don't just stand there like a cigar store, Indian. Pick up my bags, George." In those days Native Americans and blacks were only addressed as George.

Ol' Joe broke the godfather's jaw and in true Masonic fashion was transported back to Kansas. Before leaving, he would see my father one last time, who was eight years of age then.

The other doorman, Robert Wynn Sr., would be the father of the man who would become my future stepfather.

My grandmother changed my life in that conversation because up until that day I saw myself as having undergone the label change from colored to Negro to black to African American, and now I find out about my German, English, French, Dutch, Creole, and Cherokee roots.

Sandy would enroll me in anger management at the Division of Indian Works on Thirty-First and Park in South Minneapolis. I sat in a classroom with twelve natives and another black man who, like me, had native blood in his background. In the three years that I attended his classes, my teacher Larry Stillday brought out my Native American emotional issues, and I bonded with all my people. I learned the mechanics of growing, and with a reattachment to my native spirituality, I evolved on many levels.

CHAPTER
Fifty-Four

Sandy and I got married in May of 1986, and I had good intentions in this—my third marriage. Sandy was a very loving, spiritual woman who loved me deeply for the part of me that she saw as troubled but with potential. In truth, she deserved much better. I was dysfunctional, and all my inner child issues preceded my good intentions. Sandy and I got custody of my daughter Brandy, and Sandy was a mother figure and a friend to Brandy.

Sandy's father Marvin and all the members of her family displayed a lot of patience through the years, and all were very loving toward Brandy.

This period would also be a period when members of my mother's family, the Nelsons (not Ozzie, Harriett, David, and Ricky), would become blessed with a young musician, who came into prominence by a movie called *Purple Rain*. I recalled my cousin Tracy Sims (1983) telling me of a family member named Skipper, who was about to "shake up the world." Tracy was surprised that I didn't know who my cousin was.

By 1987, I had seen the rise of Prince and went to my mother and asked her why she never told me about another Skipper in the family. Her husband, Maurice, stepped in, and his explanation was that (Mattie Shaw) Prince's mother operated a brothel in North Minneapolis and that I had been shielded from that part of the family for ethical reasons.

I wondered why my mother was spending so much time with someone she referred to as Uncle John. This man never entered my home as a kid. I remembered seeing this eleven-year-old sitting on the sidelines at Bryant Junior High School in the evenings. I was twenty-one years old and was running up and down the court playing basketball and saw this kid with a huge afro hairdo sitting with Ward Mitchell's little brother. The little kids had to wait their turn to get their court time. I never saw little Skipper play because in one year I would be on my adventure to California. To my knowledge, Prince and I were the only ballers in the family.

In the summer of 1987, a girl who knew Duane Nelson, Prince's brother, told Duane about this cousin that she worked with. Duane told her to have me show up at William's Pub in uptown.

Sandy and I showed up "ragged down" (dressed to the nines) at about 8:00 p.m.

We took a table, and even though Sandy didn't drink, I ordered a Long island iced tea, which had a considerable amount of alcohol in it. It was happy hour, so the server brought two to me. After drinking both drinks, the music was starting to sound good enough to me for me to feel the need to express myself, so since Sandy didn't dance, with her permission, I asked another woman to dance with me. The two teas gave me my rhythm, and I enjoyed two songs with the woman. After the dances, I returned to the table and ordered my third tea, and after drinking enough to lose control of my logical mind, I was interrupted by two big men who told me that "someone upstairs" wanted to meet me. Sandy and I followed what turned out to be two of Prince's security guards up the stairs, and over in the corner was Duane and Prince sitting in semidarkness.

As I was ascending the steps, I believe the Long Island teas were starting to overtake my judgment because when I stood in front of Prince and Duane, reeking of alcohol, I greeted him with the unnecessary arrogance of "What's happening, Skipper?"—no respect whatsoever.

Prince wanted to know how I was related to him to which I asked him if he knew Marge Turner. When Prince acknowledged knowing his cousin Marge, I told him that I was her son. He and Duane smiled, and I was so self-absorbed that I didn't even remember to introduce Sandy as my wife. I told him that I was very proud of him, and he relaxed and accepted my compliment with a body language that revealed a shyness.

I would have been successful, but as the buffoon that I've had the unique tendency of being, I told him to be careful in Hollywood and to watch his ass. I told him of my rape in jail and didn't want him to suffer like I did.

That's when Prince's entire demeanor switched, and he nodded to the guards to take my stupid drunk ass away.

That was my first and last encounter with my namesake Skipper.

In hindsight, it was one of my deepest regrets in my life. I was a complete fool and can never get that stupid moment back. This young man would go on to become an icon in the music industry for the next forty years of his life and would write a piece entitled "The Moors in Spain."

CHAPTER
Fifty-Five

I would also begin to study the works of John Henrick Clark, Ben Jochannan, Leonard Jefferies, and Dr. Charles Finch. I would look at the conditions of the taxi industry in the Minneapolis Suburbs and devise something called Concept 90, which was a seven-step program and five-fundamental-principle teaching system to teach cabdrivers how to become sales representatives and sell the company in a uniformed manner that would build the brand. I was brilliant, but my dysfunctional personality preceded my idea—I would sell the idea to Gary the owner but sabotage the program with my behavior. I would confuse the owner with my outlandish behavior. I would graduate from my anger management classes and sign up for one-on-one therapy with Jenny Jacobs at Side by Side, a neighborhood family clinic in Bloomington, and began to explore my core emotional issues that needed to be investigated for me to begin to grow as a person. I would also begin to study John Henrick Clark (see "A Great and Mighty Walk" in YouTube), Dr. Ben Jochannan, Leonard Jefferies, and Dr. Charles Finch (*The Egyptian Genesis of Religion*, *The Pharaonic Origin of Medicine* in Youtube).

I studied the books of Gerald Massey and everything my friend Wes would tell me about. By 1988, I was growing, and the information that I was accumulating and assimilating was raising my consciousness to a level I never expected to get to, even though I knew I was on a spiritual path to knowing. Sandy and I shared custody with Brandy's mother.

As much agonizing as I had put myself through, Sandy and I provided a better lifestyle in the southwest Bloomington area than the projects on Aldrich. The factor that sealed the deal was that Brandy's mother could keep getting her welfare money.

After a few months, my overwork landed me in Golden Valley's Glenwood Hills Hospital for a week of what I refer to as coming back to reality. I had flipped out on a Suburban taxi dispatcher and quit and parked my cab. In a couple of days, Mark Muldoon, the business manager at Suburban, called and told me that he and a team of good drivers left Suburban and wanted to know if I wanted to join them at Airport Taxi, one of their competitors.

I told that I was interested, and the next day Ken Reinke was ringing my buzzer at 102nd and Normandale at 6:30 a.m.

I started out in the taxi business with Kenny at Southwest Taxi, where he literally ran the entire operation. Jim Isaacson, the owner, moved on to create Road Runner Delivery, and Kenny and a man named Robert Zimmerman created Airport Taxi Corporation. Kenny introduced me to Zimmerman, the owner, whom I kind of trained before I went back to California. Kenny had promised me a very sharp 1984 Caprice Classic, and I didn't realize how many toes I stepped on when I accepted that car.

Because of my prior relationship with Muldoon, Kenny, and Zimmerman, the owner, I was seen by the other drivers as privileged.

Airport Taxi at the time had 125 drivers, of which there were four black drivers, including me.

The two mechanics at the garage where all the lease taxis were serviced by three men with hillbilly minds prejudged me as uppity, and their white supremacy core belief system saw me as the worst kind of nigger.

Airport Taxi had a European collection of druids, neo-Nazis, white supremacists, and a few that knew me from the old days at the three other companies we worked together at.

My therapy was changing me, and Jenny and I had enough esoteric conversations for her to refer me to Marie Burgeson in St. Paul for esoteric counseling and therapy. After a few series of psychic readings, I began to study the chakra system. I began to grow by leaps and bounds, and my only problem was the white backlash at work.

It was a case of spirit warfare, and I was alone and on my own. Jenny Jacobs recommended a book to me by Marilyn Mason and

Robert Fossem called *Facing Shame*. This book was one of the keys to my transformation.

When I had studied this book, I studied the dynamics of shame. It was in 1988 when my friend advised me to "put the ancestors" on my coworkers.

Once I did this, my energy changed and I began to become grounded. Dr. James Small's (YouTube) African spiritual system taught me that by calling on the collective spirit of my ancestors all the way back to creation is a force that any perversion cannot penetrate.

European branches or versions are spiritually diluted aspects of a science that has original power. The therapy combined with the ancient knowledge of my people grounded me in so many aspects that I was growing.

CHAPTER
Fifty-Six

By 1990, I ran Sandy off again, and this time we would be separated for a year. In the time that we were separated, I had gotten esoteric therapy and studied the Hindu chakra system with Marie Burgeson. My therapist Jenny had lunch with a woman named Barbara Stamp, who was teaching in a family-related program for inmates at the Minnesota State Correctional Institute for Women in Shakopee, Minnesota. Their discussion concerned having a male abuser who had been transformed through the therapy process. Jenny brought up my case and suggested that I talk to the women.

Barbara Stamp, who ran the group, must have liked what she was seeing in the way of interaction between the women and myself because she kept referring me to other women's agencies in Minneapolis and St. Paul as a consultant. I was sent to workshops that addressed rehabilitation and support for women and men.

I was telling my story and speaking from my heart from a responsible and accountable perspective. I was going to the Shakopee Correctional Facility on a monthly basis to share my story with the new inmates to Barbara Stamp's program.

I began to speak and was invited back to the point where over a five-year period was the capstone on my personal pyramid. The women got the opportunity to hear my story, and the next day I returned for question-and-answer sessions.

I was a single working father with more emotional stability that I had ever had in my life. I got more out of going into a woman's facility and being honest about myself.

CHAPTER
Fifty-Seven

After about a year, I had lunch with my father-in-law (Marvin) and was told that Sandy had reconnected with Sonny, whom she had been with for seven years before meeting me. I told Marvin that I took responsibility for that because of my behavior. I was only being honest. About a week later, Sandy called and wanted to talk. Sandy explained that Marvin felt that the two of us hadn't ever gotten away as a couple and needed to remember each other.

I told Sandy that I had been seeing a woman for a few months but still had love for her. Sandy offered choices: Jamaica, Florida, Los Angeles, Mexico, or anywhere else. I chose Mazatlán.

This was during Easter vacation, and Brandy was with her mother.

Marvin was correct in his assumption because after two days in Mexico, Sandy got prettier and prettier. The week passed, and it was time to come back to reality.

Once our plane landed, Sandy asked to come home, and a few days later Brandy returned from her mother's home.

The reality was that I was not the same person that I had been when she left a year ago, and it became obvious to Brandy and I right away. Psychologically Sandy was very angry not only from our previous relationship, but she had had less than an ideal relationship with Sonny. Sandy needed therapy to understand what had transpired in the year that she was gone. Brandy and I had undergone therapy and were in the process of changing emotionally.

I can understand how Sandy must've felt coming back and the abuser who threw her out was giving domestic abuse prevention workshops not just at the women's prison but at other women's facilities in Hennepin and Ramsey County.

Sandy was used to being in a high stress environment, and Brandy and I had changed.

Sandy would come home from work and subconsciously "push my buttons" and get no reaction—only a response.

She became very angry and frustrated. I understood because my therapist had explained the dynamics to me. I suggested to Sandy that she get therapy, but she felt that since she had been a victim, there was no need for therapy.

This syndrome would go on for 288 days in a row, and Sandy wasn't working anymore. She somehow lost her job at Mystic Lake Casino. I didn't press Sandy for information about it because she was too sensitive about it.

One night, about 2:00 a.m., I sat down with Sandy to tell her that I had worked almost three hundred days without a day off, and between her father paying our rent and my efforts, I needed her help. At about 3:30 a.m., Sandy, who had gotten tired of the subject matter, yelled out, "WHAT DO YOU WANT ME TO DO—SELL MY ASS?"

I had a daughter on the other side of that bedroom wall that was sleeping, and I got up and ran a bubble bath and excused myself.

After about an hour, I returned and asked her to join me in the living room. I explained to her that her outburst was counterproductive to what I was trying to do with my daughter and that since she still had a bedroom at her father's house, she should go back there. I explained to her that if Brandy were her child, I would leave. I suggested that she leave at 9:00 a.m. that morning. I also explained to her that I was not going to let her take me backward in my growth.

I can say that it was the most difficult decision that I've ever made in my life and it hurt me more than anyone else. That morning I went to work and never saw Sandy again.

CHAPTER
Fifty-Eight

I went into a deep depression, and in the evenings that Brandy spent with me, I would stare out the living room window in a fog.

Brandy needed a father on an emotional level and began to take off on weekends under the guise of spending the weekends with her girlfriends. I probably should have checked the phone numbers, but I trusted Brandy.

I would later find that Brandy was hanging out in a "safe house" in East Bloomington, where a family invited wayward teenagers a safe place to hang out.

I told the mother of Brandy, and they got Brandy and took her back to her mother's house. In days they invited me to a family meeting. I drove over, and when I got there, all the members of Brandy's mother's family were there and had predecided Brandy's fate before I got there.

For more effect, Brandy was sitting on the floor at her mother's feet showing solidarity. I had tears in my eyes as my father-in-law smiled. I was crying because I knew the mistake that Brandy was making. I drove home and went even deeper into depression. Jenny, my therapist, got me through a very dark period.

I would begin bodybuilding with a friend (Joe Gelhar) and fellow driver, and in 1995 I had a none-at-fault accident and completely severed my supraspinatus muscle and lost my mobility.

I broke down emotionally and physically and spent seventy-two hours in Southdale Fairview Crisis Center and got released to go back to work. To be honest, one afternoon I picked up some men at one of the motels in Bloomington and transported them to the Mall of America. I got the same men on the return ride back to the motel. We connected, and they invited me in their rooms. We talked for about two hours and bonded because Mex means mixed, and I am certainly mixed, so I gave them my home phone number.

The next day I got a call from them to meet up with them. This time they invited me up to meet Mr. Man.

I was surprised by his size and looks. He was about six feet and two inches and weighed about 210 pounds of muscle.

He was very handsome and had a great smile.

After our conversation, he asked me if he could hire me exclusively.

The next day I picked two people up who loaded the trunk with luggage and bags. We went to places in Edina and the western suburbs that were very upscale. At the end of my day, I went home and waited for the call the next day.

After about a week, I got a call to transport them to the airport. One week later, I picked them up at the airport and took them to a townhouse in Eagan, Minnesota.

These people trusted me, and I trusted them and I knew how to act in a businesslike manner.

That Thursday, I was asked to call in the morning.

The next morning, I called, and when I asked where we were headed, I was told that we were going to Las Vegas.

By 5:00 p.m., the main man asked me if I knew where he could get a piece of cocaine.

I made a call, and we went to the home of a woman friend of mine and waited while she left to obtain what he wanted. At 7:00 p.m., the woman friend came back, and the main man told us we were going to Las Vegas. My woman friend asked her husband, and at 8:30 p.m., we were sitting on a plane about to fly to Las Vegas.

My friend was drinking tequila and got loud and was getting louder. We were in first class, and my main man thought he smelled a fart and was quite vocal about it. The noise brought a man from the coach section up to us, and this man was big (three hundred pounds).

The man told the main man to shut up because he had kids who were listening. Main man told the father that he was unaware of who he was telling to shut up and that when the plane landed, he should wait for us and his children would "see quite a show."

We landed, and we never saw the man and his kids again.

We took a cab to our plush hotel, and main man had his room with his woman.

I had a woman with me in our suite, but she was married to a man I babysat when he was very young. She had her bed, and I had mine.

Soon we were invited to join main man in his room, and the other two men came in who had just returned from Mexico.

They gave main man the boulder, and they brought out the pipe and we had a party.

We went to Caesars Palace at 2:00 a.m. and danced until sunup.

Friday and Saturday were a blur, and on Saturday night, the main man told me we were leaving for Minneapolis on Sunday, but we have to stop in Phoenix Arizona first. I knew that main man had businesses in Tucson, Arizona, so I was suspicious.

Main man invited me soon to his suite and offered me the Minnesota territory for twenty-five thousand dollars per month.

His entire demeanor changed when I told him that I wouldn't do anything that would put shame on my children.

I knew when I got the offer that I had earned his trust, but I knew when it was time to go.

I went back to the suite that I was sharing with my woman friend and told her to pack and call a cab to the airport.

I put her in a cab and phoned her husband to tell him she was on her way home.

I left and connected in Phoenix and got back to Minnesota. My cab was locked up in main man's garage. After a call to him in Las Vegas, I got them to pay a locksmith to get the cab out of the garage.

Two weeks later, I got a call from main man calling from Tucson. He had been in a shootout, and he needed $250.

In a day and one half, I wired main man his money at Western Union.

Main man called when he got the money and praised me for sending the money. He said people owe him thousands and won't pay him and promised to come to Minneapolis and buy me two cabs.

When I checked into the Southdale Fairview Crisis Center, I was a work in progress at 145 pounds. It would be my last drug party.

CHAPTER
Fifty-Nine

At forty-seven years of age, you are too old to party with anything. I was lonely and didn't feel grounded enough. I went to the psychic fair at St. Anthony Main and had a reading with Sandra that had quite an impact on me.

Sandra said that I was about to meet my soul mate. She gave me a brief description of what a soul mate was, and I asked her how I will know.

She said, "In a few weeks before you meet her, you will begin to feel a yearning and you won't know why."

Sandra added, "Look into her eyes and something will just click."

I asked, "What will she be like?"

Her answer was "Just like you. She has a tremendous amount of energy. She is lucky that you have your energy. She would have a difficult time finding someone to match her energy.

She said she doesn't realize that she's as brilliant as she is and that I would have to help her with that. She said, "I see her with a little boy who's no longer a little boy anymore. She's not far away."

CHAPTER

Sixty

I was one of the first occupants of a brand-new high-rise hotel called the Suburban Lodge. I was in Burnsville and loved the wide-open spaces. I had a kitchenette with a microwave, refrigerator, color TV, bed, and bathroom.

All I did was work, and it was around this time when my therapist Jenny Jacobs informed me that I needed to give up my time each week to someone who could use my time slot.

She told me that I had been managing my life for some time and would continue to do so.

In 1996, I would reacquaint myself with a childhood friend. I would, through him, meet Dr. Fred Clary, a chiropractor / power-lifter of world-class levels.

In 1994, Clary was fourth in the world in powerlifting. Through Dr. Clary, I repaired a supraspinatus muscle, and between my reacquainted friend and my friend Wesley McGee, I began to grow by leaps and bounds.

CHAPTER
Sixty-One

One afternoon, I was sitting on a cabstand in West Bloomington when a voice came over our dispatch system.

The voice was of a woman who said it was her first day dispatching. She asked the drivers for understanding and cooperation.

Whatever I heard in her voice made me drive across the road and go into the Lincoln Del Restaurant and call her from a pay phone.

My words were "You are going to be good. Don't let those men get in your way."

After about three weeks, I went to the office and went to the area where the dispatchers were and bluntly asked her, "When are we going out?"

Her reply was "I have a man." I was so embarrassed as I apologized to her and walked away. This was in March, and I wondered to myself what had made me call her on the phone in the first place. Not long after that, I went down to Mikal and Associates and got another reading. This time I got the reading from a woman named Claudia. I always recorded my readings on cassette to be able to compare instances later.

Claudia asked me who I got pregnant on the job. I told her that I wasn't dating anyone that I worked with. She told me that someone on my job who worked with computers would become pregnant with my child. At the time of this reading, there were no computers in the taxi business. She said I would write a book that would bring a new truth to the world. She said she saw me (symbolically) sitting at the top of a mountain speaking to the multitude of people below.

I left the reading wondering about getting someone pregnant.

I guess a couple of months went by, and one afternoon I got a fare that only went about a block and the customer was kind enough to realize that the fare was short and gave me a twenty-dollar bill and told me to keep the change. I informed the dispatcher of the short trip and asked if it cost me my place in line.

Karwyn was the dispatcher, and she said no, that I was still first up. I told her that I loved her for what she said. Her response was "You wouldn't love me if you really knew me."

I was kind of at a loss for words, and I headed for the nearest payphone and called her and asked her what she meant by that statement. She explained to me that that morning her daughter caught her live-in boyfriend trying to set up a date with another woman. She said she went home and told him to leave now.

I told her that she didn't need that loser and that we can now start going out. Her reply was the question of her needing time to grieve. I told her she didn't need time, but I gave her my phone number and told her to call.

About a week went by, and Karwyn called and told me that she thought she could "escape" and meet me.

We met at the Target parking lot on Fifty-Third and Central Avenue Northeast in Fridley.

She parked her car, and we took my car and only went a couple of blocks away to a parking lot with a church and a pond with a couple of ducks swimming in it.

We got out and looked at the ducks. She walked toward me, and I believe there was a voice from God that said, "Don't make her cry." We stood there looking at the ducks and talking.

We sat in the car for about an hour and went to get a bite to eat and came back to the same spot. Each night for about a week, we met at the same place and went to our spot and talked for hours.

There were nights when we talked until we both put our seats back and slept the night. She'd go home and to work and me the same.

One night we were sitting there talking, and a cop or security shined a flashlight in my face. He asked what we were doing. I answered that we were dating. He told us that we should move.

We decided to meet at my place in Burnsville.

She began coming to my place, and each evening she'd call and ask if she could cruise out. I was delighted each time she'd ask. She'd drive from Fridley to Burnsville, and that to me was quite a distance to drive. I was impressed.

After dinner we'd spend the evening in my room talking and watching sporting events. I enjoyed just being with her and even though there were nights that she would spend the night I made no advances toward her at all. My instincts told me that she was special.

I went to the office one day to pay my lease and went into the dispatch area to say hello to her.

Sitting on the floor was one of the most beautiful five-year-old boys I'd ever seen. He was playing something called Pokemon. I sat down with him, and since he was the one making the rules, I lost my fifty cents right away. I asked him his name and he said, "Nick."

Even though his name was Nicholas, he told me, "Just plain Nick."

Karwyn and I spent quite a bit of time together, and it was at my place where we could, as she referred to it, hang out.

Karwyn explained to me that she had four kids and had been in a very abusive relationship for seven years and that Nick's father had made serious terroristic threats toward her and her parents. At one point Karwyn had to go up north to Pequot Lakes to get away from the out-of-control ex.

After we compared notes, we both realized that she and her kids were the family that my mother and her husband were going to their church, lighting candles, and praying for.

We sat down and built a relationship around her children's needs. I didn't formally meet them for quite some time. Karwyn had never dated a black man before so this was a new experience for her.

I smiled because at the time that I met her, I was well versed in psychology, kemetology, ancient history, and the esoteric chakra system, and I had two teachers.

The first was a man who was a master body builder and was adept at, eastern and western astrology, soul-centered astrology, and he possessed an enormous amount of wisdom and knowledge of the esoteric aspects.

The other man that I was being taught by is Wesley McGee, who is a master research specialist and master of world history.

These two masterminds are the reason why I was spiritually prepared to meet Karwyn. These two men are responsible for my growth and transformation on so many levels of awareness not only of myself but of my oneness with the universe. Both of these men gave me almost daily data on their subjects of mastership, and I was able to integrate their teachings and process them at a state of super-conscious expansion.

My best friend was always Paula Carey, Warren, Aranda.

Paula and I have a respect that encompasses at least three generations.

Paula was my rock, and when I needed her, she never hesitated for a second to be there for me. It was my relationship with Paula that taught me how to be friends after ending what was an engagement and growing as friends forever. Over a thirty-plus-year period, she kept me grounded whenever I needed her. When I lost my apartment in Bloomington, Paula moved me into an apartment building that her father owned.

I told Karwyn about Paula and the friendship that we had. I wanted Karwyn to trust me. I also had a friend named Susan Peterson whose man was in prison for a year and rented Susan's basement. Karwyn trusted me.

Karwyn would drive to Woodbury to see me and go home to get her kids off to school the next day. Karwyn got pregnant, and we lost the daughter due to a miscarriage. I knew that the second daughter died due to a miscarriage and that I would never leave her.

I have a great relationship with her daughter, Jamie. Our love and respect for each other was earned and not expected for biological reasons. She has replenished all that was lost over the years with my biological children. By this I mean that my needs have been met.

The three boys had fathers, and I was never trying to replace those men. My purpose was to be an example that could be viewed over a twenty-year period that would serve two purposes: (1) to demonstrate the manner in which a man is to relate to his mate and (2) to work with Karwyn to create healing for all of us.

Karwyn's father, Lowell, told me years ago at their cabin that out of the family, she seemed to take the initiative the most. He said that Karwyn sees what needs attention and just attends to it.

It's my opinion that she does it better than anyone I've ever seen. She has passed this trait on to her children, and they are passing this on to the grandchildren. My parenting skills were almost non-existent because of my dysfunctional background. As a single parent, her dedication and loyalty to her children and anyone that she considers a friend are coming from her wonderful spirit.

Karwyn didn't need a man to raise her children because she had a vision of what she wanted for them that didn't require a man. My role in this relationship was to be there for support and to be 100 percent safe for her and all the members of her family and friends. In short, Karwyn trusted me enough to let me in her loved, protected world.

Her work ethic is unmatched, male or female, that I've seen anywhere. She would've excelled at anything she chose to do. She runs an incredible amount of energy and can run feminine and masculine energy at will.

I don't need to dwell on this because women recognize this trait. I was prepared by the Creator and the ancestors to be ready when I met Karwyn.

Because of the studies through therapy and the study of African cosmology, I was able to have the consciousness to place Karwyn (through MAAT) above me with the Father Spirit. Through the principles of MAAT, we live a totally abuse-free life, and we, the family, have healed.

Karwyn is a very special woman.

We had an understanding about our not living together for the children's sake, and we built our relationship around her children's needs.

Her children didn't want to live with any more male friends. The only time that I had spent the night at her place was after a surgery that I had when I slept on her couch. Karwyn understood the value of Nick having a relationship with his father even though she was afraid. I was so proud of this woman for risking her safety so that Nick would have access to his father.

Each time Nick's father's visitation day came, she would meet at a Burger King restaurant, and I would worry, but I had great respect for her even though I was worried.

I met her daughter at Southdale Shopping Center parking lot. Her battery needed a jump.

CHAPTER
Sixty-Two

Airport Taxi was sold to a company named Coach USA, and Karwyn became the communications manager. The Raywood computer system was installed in all the cabs. Coach bought Town Taxi and Pioneer Taxi, and our fleet increased to over five hundred taxis.

Coach had some legal problems and sold the company back to the Pints from whom they bought it from. Then the Pints bought Minneapolis Yellow Cab.

We had an influx of drivers from various countries in Africa. What had been about 90 percent Northern European drivers in number became about 90 percent African drivers overnight. This was a culture shock to say the least. Airport Taxi always had a white staff, and the operation was being run with plantation politics. By this I mean we could drive taxis but not work on staff.

To me it was amusing because I had only a few white drivers for friends, and the African drivers saw me as a Black American.

With my knowledge of African history, I was enjoying the fact that I knew more about Africans than they knew about their own history. We also had drivers from Egypt and Iran in the company who didn't see me as a legitimate Muslim because I wasn't attending their mosque.

My friend Wes gave me so much information on the African spiritual system that I had no real challengers. The white drivers were experiencing a brand-new mindset—for the first time in Minnesota taxi history they were going to work as minorities. The Africans were segregating themselves from the whites, and the whites were not enjoying the white supremacy advantage that they had had all these years.

The Nigerians were gossiping about me and were social only when I pointed out to them the fact that I was discussing their heritage with them and they were not contributing much. The drivers knew who Karwyn was and called her Momma Karwyn.

There was no one in the company that had as much experience, from driver to owner and vice president. The white staff hadn't driven a cab, and even the driver manager had no knowledge of driving a cab.

Karwyn had performed every phase of the taxi business and was given a new position to go with communication manager, which was the head of driver relations. Everyone knew that we were a couple, and the management saw her as being one of them (white) and tried to influence her to get away from me. The Africans didn't trust the whites but trusted Karwyn.

Karwyn was loyal to me, so the establishment put so much pressure on her until she began to breakdown health-wise.

I would have my income controlled to the point where I was always in the hole in owing to the company. I would borrow from my $1,500 deposit to cover my balance and paid them back twenty-five dollars per week. Airport Taxi never had a black person on staff except a dispatcher or call taker.

Racists? You bet. I saw them for what they were, and their gossip and he-said, she-said kept me in a driver position for thirty years with the company. My only flaw was that I didn't kiss anyone's butt to get promoted.

I lost my apartment because Airport Taxi got paid first.

Karwyn's health cost her her position, and she would move me in with her when Nick was nineteen years old. Eventually she had me check my social security, and she told me that I would make more money retiring. All those years of working almost every day of a 365-day year and I could barely feed myself. I never made above poverty wages. The plus was that I spent twelve to sixteen hours per day studying, and so it was worthwhile.

Karwyn and I have been together twenty-plus years, and to this day we have never had an argument. People wonder how we could accomplish such a feat.

When I studied Ptahhotep, I say what I discovered as the manner in which to treat my woman.

Also, I learned that the goddess Maat, who presided over the original Judgment Day, where she weighed your heart against a feather, was that which preceded patriarchy.

Our family spiritually operates under matriarchal law. The woman is the head of the family.

In my opinion, patriarchy has destroyed society.

In Ptahhotep's words (Maxims):

P107—a woman with a happy heart brings equilibrium.

P107—love your wife with passion.

P108—as for those who lust after women, none of their plans will succeed.

In my relationship with Karwyn, I realized that her wisdom was greater than mine, and I have trusted her and her God-given teachings.

I had a pair of parents named Charles and Shirley Martin in Minneapolis. Through the years that I knew them they taught me the successful way to be a husband to cultivate a good life.

While Charles trusted his wife entirely, they raised the family together from a matriarchal perspective. I didn't understand this as their son and son-in-law, but I have used their system in my relationship with my mate. I placed her above me next to the Father Spirit, and I totally spiritually submit to both. My spiritual daughter (Jamie) has witnessed this behavior and is the matriarch in her family, and I have seen this system has produced six children in her image.

I am at peace with all the universes in God's kingdom.

Maat has become my religion. The principles of Maat have become my way of life.

My thanks to the following people: my ex-wives and the members of their families for their kindness in the face of my private journey to equilibrium and spiritual growth, those in the network of people that were affected by my bad behavior, and my children and biological offspring that were separated by my lack of awareness in my past.

Thank you to John Lewis and Dick Gregory and Louis Hayes for sleeping in my bed and for the essence that they left for me to grow from. To Harry Bellefonte and Sidney Poitier for their contribution to man and womankind and for being the "spiritual bagmen" of the civil rights movement. To Quincy Jones for his music.

To Wesley McGee for extraordinary guidance and wisdom of his masterful teachings.

About the Author

W. E. Commodore was born and raised in Minneapolis, Minnesota, to a family that evolved into what is now known as a blended family, presenting many challenges along his journey. He was raised by people that had a strong passion for advocating for equal rights to make the world a better place. They just lost track of the effect that it had on raising a family while they had different priorities. He has always been driven by his insatiable thirst for knowledge. He has studied and researched many years on the topics of domestic violence and history. He was always trying to find an explanation of how this all got started and how it ties together. He has given lectures to inmates in the women's prison to share his knowledge, give back to the community, and help victims of domestic violence. He has always had a daily journal to document his thoughts through his transformation. For many years, he wanted to write a book to chronicle his life, especially to those affected by his journey.

CPSIA information can be obtained
at www.ICGtesting.com
Printed in the USA
BVHW032253020321
601492BV00006B/489